ANIMAL RIGHTS

Mark Rowlands

First published in Great Britain in 2013 by Hodder & Stoughton. An Hachette UK company.

First published in US in 2013 by The McGraw-Hill Companies, Inc.

This edition published 2013

Copyright © Mark Rowlands 2013

The right of Mark Rowlands to be identified as the Author of the Work has been asserted by him in accordance with the Copyright, Designs and Patents Act 1988.

Database right Hodder & Stoughton (makers)

British Library Cataloguing in Publication Data: a catalogue record for this title is available from the British Library.

Library of Congress Catalog Card Number: on file.

10 9 8 7 6 5 4 3

The publisher has used its best endeavours to ensure that any website addresses referred to in this book are correct and active at the time of going to press. However, the publisher and the author have no responsibility for the websites and can make no guarantee that a site will remain live or that the content will remain relevant, decent or appropriate.

The publisher has made every effort to mark as such all words which it believes to be trademarks. The publisher should also like to make it clear that the presence of a word in the book, whether marked or unmarked, in no way affects its legal status as a trademark.

Every reasonable effort has been made by the publisher to trace the copyright holders of material in this book. Any errors or omissions should be notified in writing to the publisher, who will endeavour to rectify the situation for any reprints and future editions.

Typeset by Cenveo® Publisher Services.

Printed and bound in Great Britain by CPI Group (UK) Ltd., Croydon, CR0 4YY.

Hodder & Stoughton policy is to use papers that are natural, renewable and recyclable products and made from wood grown in sustainable forests. The logging and manufacturing processes are expected to conform to the environmental regulations of the country of origin.

Hodder & Stoughton Ltd

338 Euston Road

London NW1 3BH

www.hodder.co.uk

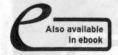

Also available in ebook

For Emma

Contents

It's not rocket science

'It is one thing to take a chainsaw to a living tree. It is quite another to take it to a living dog.'

▶ The story of a dog and a pig

When he was a little boy, my father had a dog – a German shepherd named Rex. He was very fond of the dog and would ride around the garden on its back. Around the same time, the Rowlands family also had a pig. History does not record the name of this pig, and perhaps it never had a name. But, nameless or not, my father was very fond of it and would ride around the garden on its back. Rex, by all accounts, lived a long and happy life. Things went a little differently for the pig. I relate this story not only because it provided my first brush with the idea of animal rights ('What happened to the pig, Dad?') but also because, if you look closely enough, you will find the basic moral case for animals encapsulated tightly within it.

Ethics is many things, but it's hardly rocket science. In the end, most of it is pretty obvious. The moral case for animals, as I shall try to convince you, is about as obvious as you can get. It is about as obvious as this: the differential treatment of Rex and pig is a bit strange. If we wanted to inject a little consistency into our dealings with animals, it seems we might go one of two ways. We might start treating Rex more like the pig, or the pig more like Rex. More than a few countries have embraced the first option: raising dogs in cages for food, sometimes boiling them alive because it is thought to improve the taste of their flesh, or beating them to death to release blood into the meat (Daily Mail 2012). As you might have guessed, in a book entitled *Animal Rights: All*

That Matters, I am going to run with the second option – treating the pig more like Rex. That is, I am going to develop the moral case for animals. This is sometimes called the case for *animal rights* – hence the title of the book – but actually, in developing my case, I shall hardly mention the idea of rights. People sometimes pretend not to understand talk of rights – 'What is a right, exactly? Tell me.' Well, I could tell you, but I don't need to. And so, because I have a strict word limit to contend with when writing this book, I won't (but see Feinberg 1970).

▶ Animals count

To begin at the beginning: *animals count, morally speaking.* It is one thing to take a chainsaw to a living tree. It is quite another to take it to a living dog. I mean to denigrate neither trees nor those who hug them. Continuing with the theme of things in my father's garden on which he used to climb, there was a huge horse chestnut tree, and the young me was heartbroken – and not just because of the implications for my conker supply – when it was eventually cut down on the rather flimsy grounds that it was about to fall on the house. Let's accept that trees are great. Nevertheless, taking a chainsaw to one of them is not the same as taking it to a dog or pig. Good and bad things can happen to trees. But these are all things to which trees are completely oblivious. Trees can neither suffer nor enjoy the things that happen to them. (Some people claim that they can, but they don't really have any supporting evidence.) Animals – at least, many of them – are sentient. They have a conscious life, and things can go well or badly for them in an experiential sense. They consciously enjoy the good things and consciously suffer the bad. It is why we have laws prohibiting cruelty to animals but not to trees. Implicit in these laws is the idea that one can do morally bad things to animals. If so, animals count, morally speaking.

> 'The assumption that animals are without rights, and the illusion that our treatment of them has no moral significance, is a positively outrageous example of Western crudity and barbarity. Universal compassion in the only guarantee of morality.'
>
> *Arthur Schopenhauer, German philosopher*

I won't labour this point (any more than I already have) because that would be to labour the obvious. If a man spends his time, say, electrocuting puppies then, in the absence of a rather compelling reason, most people would agree that he is doing something morally wrong. And it is morally wrong not simply because of the adverse impact it might have on the future development of the man's character. It is wrong *because of what he does to the puppies*, not because of what he does to himself. Most people, at least those whose proclivities don't run towards the psychopathic, would accept this claim. Animals count, morally speaking. Nevertheless, I shall try to show that many things follow from this obvious principle – things that, to many, will be strange and unexpected.

Notice that all I have claimed so far is that animals count, morally speaking. They have some sort of moral status. I haven't claimed – nor will I claim – that they count *as much as* human beings. People often say things like this to me: 'There's a burning building, and inside are a baby and a dog. You can save only one. Which would you save? C'mon, which would you save?' Their idea is that, if you think animals and humans count equally, you would have no basis for saving the baby over the dog. Essentially, it's a toss-up, and that seems morally deplorable. So, let me make it clear that I have not claimed that animals count as much as humans – that they are of equal moral standing. And, while we are at it, let me affirm my general commitment to saving babies should they become trapped in burning buildings from which I am able to extricate them. I have not claimed that animals count as much as humans, morally speaking, because, among other things, I don't need to claim this (essentially, the same strategy is adopted in Zamir 2007). All of the consequences I want to defend – consequences far-reaching, wide-ranging and, in many respects, world-changing – follow from the weaker claim that animals count morally, even if they don't count as much as humans do. The next step in the development of the moral case involves understanding just what it means to count, morally speaking.

To avoid using the expression '...count, morally speaking' over and over again, here is a term devised by philosophers, as useful as it is ugly: *moral considerability*. To say that something is morally considerable is just to say that it counts, morally speaking. I shall switch between the two alternate locutions to avoid unnecessary tedium. If you are morally considerable then, among other things, you will have interests that should, morally speaking, be taken into account when others are planning courses of action that impact on you. Both puppies and babies have interests in not being electrocuted, and not being consumed by burning buildings, and it is incumbent on people to take these interests into account when they start playing with live wires or matches. That is, in part, what it means for babies and puppies to be morally considerable.

▶ Vital and non-vital interests

There is one implication of being morally considerable that is particularly important for the moral case for animals. To understand this implication, we need to understand the difference between vital and non-vital interests. Your vital interests correspond to needs that must be met if you are to have anything like a rewarding or happy life. Obviously, you will need things such as food, water and shelter – without these you will die, and you can hardly live a happy life if you are dead. So, life and the conditions of life are among one's vital interests. Almost as obviously, if your life is to be remotely rewarding, you will need things like health and bodily safety and/or integrity. Your life is not going to go well if you are subject to repeated violent attacks that result in physical or emotional harm. Moreover, life as a slave is not, for humans, a decent one, and so you need the ability to pursue happiness – your conception of how you would like your life to go – free from unjustified coercion or restraint. These are all plausible examples of human vital interests. They also apply, with minor modifications, to animals.

Non-vital interests correspond to needs that do not need to be met for you to have a decent life, even though meeting these needs might increase your overall happiness: mansions, yachts and Ferraris are obvious examples. So, too, is money – as long as a certain threshold is met. No one, I assume, wants to spend their life panhandling. But after you've made your first billion, it would be difficult to make the case that your vital interests require that you now make the next. How much money is enough is, of course, subject to dispute. We don't need to get involved.

The distinction between vital and non-vital interests is a clear one. Sometimes, disputes arise over which interest falls into which camp. However, as we shall see, the moral case for animals does not require fine discriminations or contestable judgements about which interests are vital and which are not. When we examine the human treatment of animals, whether we are talking about vital or non-vital interests is – to resume an earlier refrain – entirely obvious.

With the distinction between vital and non-vital interests in hand, here is the important implication of the idea of moral considerability. If you are morally considerable – if you count, morally speaking – this precludes the sacrifice of your vital interests if this is done merely to promote the non-vital interests of others. A person can be morally considerable but not treated as such. The victims of the Nazi gas chambers were morally considerable, but not treated as such by their captors. If someone were to sacrifice your most vital interests in order to promote their own non-vital

▲ Typically we perceive animals as *useful objects*. In the headlong pursuit of our own non-vital interests – here our desire for dairy products – are we riding roughshod over the vital interests of animals?

counterparts they would be treating you as if you were not morally considerable – even though you are.

To make this abstract description more concrete, imagine the following scenario. You wake up in a hospital bed to find that your kidneys have been removed (without your knowledge or consent). The following discussion takes place between you and your assailant.

> **You:** *W-W-Why?*
>
> **Kidney thief:** *Your kidneys will fetch a tidy sum on the organ black market, and I need a new Ferrari.*
>
> **You:** *But my life is going to suck now!*
>
> **Kidney thief:** *You're probably right. I gather you will be spending much of it on dialysis – unless you can find yourself some new kidneys, of course. Speaking of...*
>
> **You:** *But, but ... don't I count, morally speaking?*
>
> **Kidney thief:** *Of course, you do. It's not as if I did this for no reason, or even for fun. I take no pleasure in illegal organ harvesting. But the new model 458 Italia really is exquisite. My life is going to be so much better now that I have it.*

I think, at this point, you should take the kidney thief's assurance that you count morally with a pinch of salt. That assurance is a sham. He is sacrificing a vital interest of yours for the sake of a non-vital interest of his – and that is tantamount to the admission that you don't, in his eyes, really count at all.

Contrast this scenario with another in which your kidneys were removed, again without your knowledge or consent, to be given to the thief's sister, who also has vital need of them. In this case, we are dealing with the sacrifice of your vital interests for the sake of the vital interests of another. This does not make it morally right – of course, it's not. But we might be more willing to accept the thief's assurance that you do count morally. It is just that you don't, in his eyes, count as much as the sister. However, in the original scenario, when your interests are sacrificed to satisfy the clearly non-vital interests of another, there is no real substance to the claim that you are being treated as if you count morally. The thief is treating you as if you do not count, morally speaking – as if you are not morally considerable. But you are morally considerable. That is why the thief's action is wrong.

We have arrived at the moral case for animals advertised at the beginning of this chapter. It is – as advertised – simple and obvious. First, animals count, morally speaking. They are morally considerable: they have interests that should, morally speaking, be taken into account when we do things that impact on them. Second, if animals count morally, we should not sacrifice their vital interests to promote the non-vital interests of others (such as ourselves). If we do this, we are treating them as if they do not count, morally speaking. Therefore, if we do this, we are doing something that is morally wrong.

This is not all there is to morality, of course. Morality has many different layers, suffused with different ideas and guiding principles. But this is the facet of morality that is, in my view, most relevant to the moral case for animals. Whenever we sacrifice the vital interests of animals to promote our own non-vital counterparts, we are doing something that is morally wrong. We are doing something wrong because we are treating an individual that does count morally as if it does not count morally. It does not follow from this, of course, that it is legitimate to sacrifice the vital interests of someone to promote one's own, or someone else's, vital interests. If the kidney thief stole your kidneys in order to give them to his sister – whom misadventure had robbed of her own – then that would also be wrong. But it would be wrong for different reasons – reasons that are not germane to the moral case for animals.

The sacrifice of the vital interests of animals to promote the non-vital interests of humans is something that goes on all the time and everywhere. Hardly any corner of the human world is exempt. Generally, our dealings with animals are not even like the second transplant scenario – where the vital interests of one person are overridden for the vital interests of another. If it were, we could hold on to the idea that we treat animals as if they count – merely not as much as we do. Rather, we override the most vital interests of animals in order to promote relatively trivial interests of our own. In our dealings with animals, we treat them as if they don't count. This is, first and foremost, a moral failure on our part. If we are to rectify this, the way we treat animals must change dramatically. That is the subject of the rest of this book. But, first, there is some unfinished business.

2

Why animals count

'...there is no relevant difference between humans and (at least some) animals that could give moral status to the former and deny it to the latter.'

In developing the moral case for animals, I relied on a premise that I didn't really spend much time defending because I think that most people will readily accept it. The premise is that animals count, morally speaking. I didn't claim that they count as much as we do – whatever that means. I simply claimed that they count: that they have some sort of moral status. It is difficult to imagine who would want to deny this. Someone who tortures kittens and puppies for fun is, it seems, doing something morally wrong. He/she will also attract considerable attention from law-enforcement agencies on the grounds that people who torture animals often go on to do the same to humans. But implications for the person's future actions are not the only – or even primary – reason why what he/she does is wrong. It is wrong because of the harm done to the puppies/kittens. If you want to deny that animals count morally, then you are committed to the claim that the kitten/puppy torturer is, in fact, doing nothing wrong.

Of course, some people might endorse this claim. What can one say to those people? More than that, there is an interesting theoretical question: if animals count, morally speaking, why is it that they count? If you believe that animals do count morally, and are uninterested in the theoretical question of why this is so, you might want to skip to the next chapter. If you are really not sure that animals count morally at all, or if you want to understand why they do, then read on.

Here is a principle that, in the domain of moral philosophy – where it sometimes seems that everything can be questioned – is as about as unassailable as a principle can get: *no moral difference without some relevant other difference.* Consider someone who is morally evil. History provides a large repository of possible examples, but philosophers always seem to plump for Hitler. So let's work with him. What made Hitler morally evil? Some claim that it was what he did: his actions made him evil. Others claim that it must have at least something to do with his motives or intentions, and not simply his actions. We don't need to get involved in this dispute. Imagine someone – we'll call them 'Schicklgrüber' – who does the same sorts of things as Hitler, and does them for the same reasons, motives or intentions. It would make no sense to claim that, whereas Hitler is evil, Schicklgrüber is not. This is the principle, 'no moral difference without some other relevant difference' at work. If they both do the same sorts of things for the same sorts of reasons, then there is no morally relevant difference between Hitler and Schicklgrüber. Therefore, if Hitler is evil, Schicklgrüber must be evil too. Conversely, if Hitler were evil and Schicklgrüber not, there would have to be some relevant difference between them. Not all differences need be relevant. If Schicklgrüber were female, this would not alter her evilness. Nor does it matter where and when Schicklgrüber carries out his/her atrocities. If they took place in East Asia instead of Europe, and in the twenty-first century rather than the twentieth, this would not alter our moral evaluation of him/her.

In addition to people, we can also morally evaluate other things: actions, rules, policies, practices and institutions can all be assessed as good or bad, right or wrong. The principle 'no moral difference without some relevant other difference' applies to them all. This principle lies at the heart of morality – and also of the case for animal rights. To explain why, recall the idea of moral considerability, introduced in the previous chapter. Something is morally considerable if it counts morally: if it has interests that, morally speaking, should be taken into consideration. What is and what is not morally considerable is also governed by the principle 'no moral difference without some relevant other difference'.

Consider my favourite example of something that is morally considerable – me! I count, morally speaking. People should, morally speaking, take into consideration the way their actions will impact on me. But, if I count, morally speaking, then I am going to have to allow, however grudgingly, that other people do, too. This is because, as far as I can tell, there is no relevant difference between them and me. In all general and relevant respects, other people are just like me. If I count morally, they do, too. The idea central to the democratic tradition – that we are born equal and have certain inalienable rights that cannot be overridden no matter how tempting, convenient or fun it might be to do so – can be derived from the claim that I count and that there are no relevant differences between me and anyone else.

▶ Three premises...

Putting these ideas together, we arrive at the idea that animals are morally considerable – at least, they are if humans are. Here is the argument.

First premise: *Humans count, morally speaking.*

That is, humans are morally considerable. This seems to be a pretty safe premise to me. Some psychopaths might reject this claim – but you can't argue morally with psychopaths. I'll assume the typical reader of this book does not fall into that category.

> **Second premise:** *If humans count morally but animals do not, there must be some relevant difference between them.*

Again, this seems a safe bet: it is simply an application of the principle 'no moral difference without some relevant other difference' to the idea of moral considerability. The principle is foundational to morality, and there is little change to be had out of contesting it.

Now we come to the big one.

> **Third premise:** *On the matter of moral considerability, there is no morally relevant difference between humans and (many) other animals.*

This is not, of course, to claim that there are no differences between humans and other animals. It is not even to claim that there are no morally relevant differences between them and us. Rather, the claim is that there is no difference between humans and (many – obviously not all) *other animals of a sort that could justify the claim that whereas humans count morally animals do not.* Obviously, this is the premise that requires defence – a lot of it. If this defence can be successfully mounted, we would arrive at the conclusion of the argument:

> **Conclusion:** *Therefore, (many) animals count morally.*

I shall examine what this claim means shortly. First, I'll defend the controversial third premise.

There are, of course, many differences between humans and other animals. No one denies this. The question is whether these differences are relevant to moral considerability. That is, are the differences between humans and other animals enough to make the former morally considerable while denying that status to the latter? Intelligence is the difference most commonly cited as the decisive difference between humans and other animals. If it is, then we would count morally, and they would not, because we are smarter than them. Is level of intelligence morally relevant? That is, could difference in intelligence justify the claim that, whereas humans count morally, animals do not?

It is very unlikely that it can. It may be true that *most* humans are more intelligent than *most* animals, but it is not true of *all* humans. The study of animal intelligence is still in its infancy. But there are certain broad categories of humans whose members, it seems likely, fall short of the intelligence of some animals. Most obviously, there are infants and young children (under about 18 months of age). My eldest son was one year old when we acquired a German shepherd puppy. They developed together, intellectually speaking, and for the next six months it was neck-and-neck. Of course, one might claim – correctly – that my son always had more intellectual potential than our dog. While true, appeals to potential are tricky. Potential abilities only give you potential claims to things. For example, being born in the US, my sons have the potential to be US President. Unfortunately, this does not give them the actual claims of the President – which is unfortunate because Air Force One would be distinctly useful on those expeditions we laughingly call 'summer holidays'. If intelligence were the key to moral considerability – which is the proposal now under examination – then appeal to potential intelligence would give you only potential moral considerability. And, anyway, appeals to potential don't even apply in all cases. Some humans with severe brain damage or with degenerative brain disorders also fall short of the intelligence of some animals. The same may be true of some humans with severe mental illness. While these categories are broad ones, and there is considerable variation within each category, the blanket claim that all humans are more intelligent than all animals is simply not true. What do we say about those humans that fall short in the intelligence stakes?

'If we cut up beasts simply because they cannot prevent us and because we are backing up our own side in the struggle for existence, it is only logical to cut up imbeciles, criminals, enemies or capitalists for the same reason.

C. S. Lewis, Northern Irish writer and academic'

It seems that there are two available options. The first is to deny that these humans count, morally speaking. They are not morally considerable – and so we can, without moral condemnation, do whatever we like to them. This claim is, of course, deeply counterintuitive. We can highlight its implausibility by way of what I shall call the 'Buffalo Bill Objection'. Buffalo Bill was the serial killer in the film *The Silence of the Lambs* who liked to make vestments out of human skins (donated from very unwilling victims, it goes without saying). The first option – denying that people in the categories listed above are morally considerable – entails that, if Buffalo Bill had confined his skin acquisition activities to infants, young children, those with brain damage, those with degenerative brain disorders and those with severe mental illness, then he would have done nothing morally wrong, and Jodie Foster would have had no (moral) business in hunting him down. The idiocy of this suggestion is, I assume, evident to all.

The second – markedly less psychopathic – option is to accept that these humans are morally considerable. This answer commits us to rejecting the idea that level of intelligence is the decisive factor in determining whether an individual is morally considerable. But, if it is not the decisive factor in determining whether an individual is morally considerable, neither can it be the morally decisive difference that ensures that humans count morally but that animals do not.

The same sort of argument applies to other features that are often put forward as candidates for the decisive

▲ The badger has come to symbolize our conflicted relationship with animals – dangerous carrier of TB or loveable denizen of the wild? Both images tend to obscure badgers' vital interests.

morally relevant difference between humans and other animals: use of language or tools, rationality of a certain specified sort, and so on. For all these candidate differences we can find humans who do not measure up, and so we either have to abandon the idea that the difference is decisive or go all Buffalo Bill on them. This argument – often called the *argument from marginal cases* – applies to all candidate morally relevant differences between humans and other animals, except one.

There is one remaining difference: we are human and they are not. The property of being human is one that all and only humans have, so it does not fall under the scope of the argument from marginal cases. This suggestion would allow us to circumvent the argument from marginal cases: bringing infants, young children, those with brain damage and degenerative brain conditions and so on under the moral umbrella, on the straightforward grounds that they are human. Is this – we are human and they are not – a morally relevant difference? Is it the sort of difference that could underwrite the claim that, while humans count morally, animals do not? This is implausible. Being human is a biological property, and biological properties are generally not morally relevant ones. For example, the idea that being male, or being white, gives you extra moral entitlements is not very popular these days. Moreover, would we want to deny moral status to our favourite extra-terrestrial or artificial intelligence – Spock, ET, Data, take your pick – simply because they are not human? There may be no extra-terrestrials or artificial intelligences, but this does not matter. The point is that, if there were such individuals, we, presumably, would not want to simply rule out the possibility that they might be morally considerable just because they were not human.

We can make this point graphic by way of what philosophers call a 'thought experiment' – an imaginative scenario whose function is to make an abstract idea concrete. The case of the kidney thief presented in Chapter 1 was a thought experiment. Here is another one. Suppose you are not what you think you are. Your heritage is distinctly alien. A bit like Superman – except without the superpowers – you arrived here as a baby in a pod. You look human on the outside, but on the inside you are quite different – decidedly non-human, in fact.

You have no recollection of your life before your arrival on Earth, and so you believe you are a normal human being, living a normal life. One day, medical investigation reveals the truth. No doubt this would come as bit of a shock. But there is still a clear sense in which you are the same person you always were. You must revise the biological category to which you belong, but it is still you in there. Would you be willing to say: 'OK, I don't count morally after all.' This, again, seems counterintuitive. What makes you count morally is not the biological category to which you belong but other things – your mental life, your ability to think, feel, suffer and enjoy. They are all candidates for what makes you morally considerable. Your biological species, in itself, is not.

No one yet has been able to identify any realistic candidate for the morally decisive difference that distinguishes humans from animals – a difference that would justify the claim that, whereas humans count morally, animals do not. The most likely explanation of this failure – certainly the default assumption – is that there is no such difference. If this is correct, if we count morally – and I assume we do – so, too, do at least some other animals.

▶ ...And a conclusion

That concludes the defence of premise 3 – the claim that there is no relevant difference between humans and (at least some) animals that could give moral status to the former and deny it to the latter. The conclusion that follows from premises 1, 2 and 3 taken together is that (some) animals count morally. This does not mean that animals have the same set of rights as humans, or that they should be treated in the same way. What would this even mean? Pigs get the right to vote, cows have the right to an education? What it means is that it is incumbent on us to take their interests into account. And this means that it is not morally legitimate to routinely and systematically sacrifice their vital interests to promote our non-vital interests. If we do that, we are not, in fact, taking their interests into account. We are treating them as if they do not count, morally speaking, when – as we have now demonstrated – they do count. This treatment is, therefore, morally wrong. This is the cornerstone of the moral case for animals. In the remainder of the book we shall examine the implications of this case.

First, however, there is yet more unfinished business. What do we say to someone who is unconvinced that animals have interests – at least, not in the morally relevant sense? The person I have in mind thinks that animals have interests only in the same way that plants do. This is because animals are just like plants. They are not conscious. They do not have minds. This is a view that has attracted some very well-known thinkers in the past and that still has adherents today. If (like me) you think it is a silly view, you might want to skip Chapter 3 and go straight to Chapter 4 – unless you want to know how to respond to the animal consciousness naysayers. I can't skip, of course – I have to write the next few pages. But, in recognition of the silliness of view to which I'm responding, I will keep it as brief as possible.

3

What is it with aliens and their probes?

> *'The question is not Can they reason? Nor is it Can they talk? but Can they suffer?'*
>
> *Jeremy Bentham*

▶ A thought experiment

I'm in a spot of bother: I've been abducted by aliens, apparently. Initially, I was a little offended. It is well known that aliens focus their abducting activities on the margins of society: the lonely, the dispossessed, the outsiders... the weirdos. I know I can be a bit strange sometimes, but really? After a while, however, my indignation turned to fear. It seems they are planning to conduct some rather invasive experiments on me. What is it with aliens and their probes? At the moment, as far as I can tell, they are trying to work out whether they should bother with pain relief. They are not convinced, you see. Not convinced that I can feel, suffer or enjoy the things that happen to me. They are not convinced that I am a conscious being. Rather, they are tempted by the idea that I am merely a biological machine whose behaviour can be explained without supposing that I have anything like a mind or conscious experiences. 'Don't multiply entities beyond necessity,' or so their scientists say. If they can explain my behaviour without assuming I am conscious, or have a mind of any sort, then their default assumption will be that I am not conscious. So, my project today, a rather urgent one, is to convince them that I – Mark Rowlands – have a mind.

My first step, a rather obvious one, is to protest my minded status. 'I can think, I can feel,' I tell them. However, this strategy is less efficacious than I might have hoped. All my alien captors hear is a series of unintelligible grunts. It dawns on me that I had better hope that their standards of proof are not too high. You can't really prove that anyone else has a mind – if by 'prove' you mean 'establish beyond a shadow of a doubt' – whether they belong to your species or not. The humans with whom I shared my life prior to my abduction, I love them dearly. I'm convinced that they have minds, that they are the subjects of conscious experiences, and that they can suffer or enjoy the things that happen to them. But I can't strictly prove it. It is always possible that they were, for example, sophisticated but unfeeling biological robots sent to spy on me by the aliens. This is not a possibility I take seriously, largely because I'm not insane. But it is not a possibility I can rule out beyond a shadow of a doubt. I can't prove that the robot scenario is not true. Proof is not possible with these sorts of things. The best we can do is show where the preponderance of evidence points. We might think of it as proof beyond reasonable doubt. Let's hope we agree on what's reasonable.

The aliens proceed with a set of behavioural tests to ascertain my conscious status. These basically involve inflicting various forms of minor bodily damage on me. They note that when they stick pins in me, I behave in ways fairly similar to the ways in which they would behave if pins were stuck in them. My unintelligible gibbering reaches a crescendo. After the first pin or two, I become seemingly agitated when pins are waved around in my vicinity, and try to withdraw the body parts where the pins are usually stuck. If I am unsuccessful in this, I might subsequently inhibit motion in the body part where the pin has been stuck, and so on and so forth. My behaviour supports the hypothesis that I am conscious of what is in my environment, that I will feel pain and have other unpleasant experiences when this environment impinges on me in certain ways. I have, in other words, passed the first – behavioural – test for consciousness.

Next, the aliens proceed to neurological investigation. Thankfully, these investigations are not as invasive as they might have been with inferior technology. They take a good look at my brain, using MRI, CAT, PET and SPECT scans, and so on. They discover, perhaps to their surprise, that my brain is rather like theirs – in both its overall structure and its functional profile. There are differences, of course. My cerebral cortex is not as large as theirs. But the other areas all look very similar, and tests show a broad homology of function. That is, in general, the functions performed by a given area in my brain are also performed by the corresponding area in theirs. Broadening their investigation beyond neurophysiology and neuroanatomy, they also discover certain pertinent neurochemical similarities. For example, when they stick pins in me, my brain releases endogenous opiates. Their brains do the same thing when they suffer bodily damage, and the function of these chemicals, they have surmised, is to temporarily mask pain – to enable them to flee whatever is causing the damage. Why, they speculate, would I have the ability to produce these pain-alleviating chemicals if I could not actually feel pain? So far, so good.

Intrigued by these similarities between us, the aliens decide to focus on my genetic structure. They are astonished to discover that they and I share over 95 per cent of our genes, confirming a hypothesis promulgated by some of their scientists that their species and mine share a common evolutionary ancestor. Our evolutionary histories, it appears, diverged only very recently. The alien scientists are, of course, utterly convinced that they have minds and conscious experiences. Given that our evolutionary heritage overlaps to such a great extent, they are grudgingly forced to concede that the same is probably true of me also.

▶ Animal consciousness

The thought experiment described above is, in so many ways, a silly one. I am using it to make a point – or, rather, two points. The first point is the obvious one. The evidence that could be used to establish to sceptical aliens that I am conscious is the same as the evidence that could be used to establish that animals are conscious. The evidence is of three general sorts: behavioural, neurological and evolutionary. The things that were true of me in the above thought experiment are also true of many other animals. The behavioural, neurological and evolutionary evidence supports the claim that animals are conscious to the same extent that it supports the claim that I am conscious. This is exactly the evidence that can be used to establish that animals other than humans are conscious and have minds.

In 2012 the neurological evidence, in particular, led a group of prominent neuroscience researchers, including Christof Koch, David Edelman and Philip Low, to sign the Cambridge Declaration on Consciousness.

This emphatically supported the idea that animals are conscious. Its conclusion stated:

> *non-human animals have the neuroanatomical, neurochemical, and neurophysiological substrates of conscious states along with the capacity to exhibit intentional behaviours. Consequently, the weight of evidence indicates that humans are not unique in possessing the neurological substrates that generate consciousness. Non-human animals, including all mammals and birds, and many other creatures, including octopuses, also possess these neurological substrates.* (Quoted in Bekoff 2012)

▲ Jeremy Bentham – an early proponent of animal rights.

The second point derives from the fact that the thought experiment is, patently absurd. It is difficult to take seriously in a way that is, I think, significant. There is a problem in philosophy known as the *problem of other minds*. How do you know that anyone else, apart from you, has a mind? How do you know, for example, that everyone else is not simply a cleverly constructed biological robot, ingeniously programmed to respond to you in seemingly intelligent ways? You could stick them in an MRI scanner, but how often do you have one of those handy? And, anyway, the results would be inconclusive. How do you know that activity occurring in their brain correlates with the same mental processes as activity in yours? This is the problem of other minds. Putting them in an MRI scanner merely relocates the problem but doesn't solve it.

That other humans are mindless automata is not very likely, you might think – and I would agree with you. But, there again, as far as I can see, neither is the claim that animals are mindless automata very plausible. We cannot, without justification, hold the question of animal minds up to a higher standard of proof than the question of other human minds. We cannot prove beyond a shadow of a doubt that other animals are conscious. But neither can I prove beyond a shadow of a doubt that any other human is conscious. What we have in both cases – human and animal – is the same. The preponderance of evidence – behavioural, neurological and evolutionary – strongly supports the claim that other humans and many animals are conscious.

There are theoretical problems and there are practical attitudes, and sometimes the two just don't mesh very well at all. (The eighteenth-century Scottish philosopher David Hume is well known for making this point (Hume 1975).) The problem of other minds is a genuine theoretical problem. No one has really ever solved it in the sense of conclusively proving that other humans have minds. The claim that they do is a hypothesis supported by the best available evidence. That is the most we can do from a theoretical standpoint. But to allow this theoretical attitude to intrude into our practical attitudes would be a sign of incipient madness. I don't really doubt that other humans have minds. It's not as if I think my wife and children probably have minds: that the claim that they do is a hypothesis best supported by the preponderance of evidence. If I did think that, there would be something wrong with me. I really would be a good candidate for alien abduction if I thought like this. In my everyday practical attitudes, I am certain that my human family members have minds. I am just as certain that the family dog has one, too. To suppose otherwise is just silly.

The philosopher Jeremy Bentham once wrote that, with respect to animals, 'The question is not Can they reason? Nor is it Can they talk? but Can they suffer?' Once you are a conscious, or sentient, being, you have interests and can suffer because of them. It does make sense to talk of trees having interests: interests in having access to water and sunlight, interests in not being cut down, and so on. But trees are oblivious to these interests and whether or not they are satisfied. Being sentient, animals have interests in an entirely different way. They have interests whose satisfaction they consciously enjoy and whose thwarting they consciously suffer. In this respect, at least, they have interests in the same way that humans have interests. Since animals are morally considerable, we are morally obliged to take those interests into account. And when those interests are vital, we must not, morally speaking, allow them to be sacrificed for the non-vital interests of others – even if we are among those others. The rest of the book examines the implications of this.

4

Morally wrong and terminally stupid

'Remaining alive ... is a vital interest of animals, just as it is a vital interest of humans.'

If animals are morally considerable – if they count, morally speaking – then it is morally wrong to allow their vital interests to be sacrificed to promote our non-vital interests. This means that the case against eating animals is open and shut. It's not even close. That is what I am going to argue in this chapter. The case against eating animals has two strands. The first shows that the most vital interests of animals are routinely violated in the process of raising and killing them for food. The second shows that there are no similarly vital human interests that might be promoted by the eating of meat.

▶ The life of Pig

Let us begin with the first strand: the vital interests of animals that are routinely violated in the practice of raising and killing them for food. Since this book began with a nameless pig, I shall focus on the lives of the pigs we eat. This is not the place to detail the horrors of the lives and deaths of poultry, cattle and the other creatures that find their way on to our plates – these horrors have been detailed by many others and are, by now, quite well known. I assure you that the story I am going to tell of pigs is repeated, at least in its general contours, for these other creatures.

In so many respects, my father's pig was, its untimely demise notwithstanding, rather lucky. Born a few generations later, its life would likely have been very different. Born today, it is probable that it will be raised in what is called a total-confinement farm system.

Far from charging around the garden with a child on its back, it will never see the light of day – until it is sent for slaughter at the ripe old age of five months. Let me introduce, in italics, an imaginary, but all too typical, farmer – let's call him Mr P. Farmer:

> *When it's born, I'll give it a battery of injections, clip its needle teeth (i.e. cut them down to gum level), notch its ears for identification, and cut its testicles and tail off (without anaesthetic – that would cost me money). The teeth and tail clipping are entirely necessary, I assure you: the reasons will emerge shortly. Then I shall move it for 'finishing' to a large building, divided into pens. It will share this building with several thousand other pigs until it is slaughtered.*

Pigs are intelligent, social and, contrary to widespread hominid slander, cleaner than many humans. If raised in more natural surroundings, they would likely form a stable social group, spending their time in communal nests, rooting around at the edge of riparian woodlands, and using dunging areas well away from the nest. Mr Farmer comments:

> *None of this is possible under its present regime. To prevent the build-up of a mountain of excrement, a raised, slatted floor – somewhat like a cattle grid – has been installed. This is uncomfortable (the point of cattle grids is that animals don't want to walk on them), and would eventually lead to deformity if the pig lives long enough. But, don't worry, it won't.*

Being a naturally intelligent creature, it would seem that unremitting boredom is the pig's lot. It can eat, sleep, stand up or lie down. And that is it – the entire gamut of available activities:

> *I could, I suppose, provide it with bedding materials, with which it might build a nest. But this would complicate the task of cleaning. That is, I will have to employ more people to do the cleaning, and that would be unprofitable.*

Together with its fellows, the pig will almost certainly suffer stress – perhaps it might even die from it. The symptoms of porcine stress syndrome (PSS) include rigidity, skin problems, panting and sudden death. The pig may also acquire certain stress-related vices.

> *Yes, the reason for the teeth and tail clipping now becomes clear. I told you it would. Back in the days when pigs raised in these conditions actually had tails, they started biting them – not their own, each other's – an activity that would often escalate into fighting. This must be discouraged. First, fighting is a strenuous activity. It reduces weight gain, and I will have to feed the pig more to produce the same amount of pork or bacon. Second, the tail biting would often escalate into a form of cannibalism – literally eating into my profits.*

The cause of this aggressive, cannibalistic behaviour is multi-factorial, but stress, overcrowding and boredom are centrally implicated. It has been shown, conclusively, that providing even rudimentary items such as straw bedding will substantially reduce the incidence of tail biting, owing, in part, to the recreational possibilities provided by the straw.

> *Yes, but as I said, this would make cleaning the pens more difficult – I refer you back to the earlier employment/profitability issue – and active pigs put on weight more slowly than bored ones, and thus require more feed. Therefore, my preferred method for combating tail biting is far more simple and direct: clip the teeth and cut off the tail. Hence, also, the total confinement under reduced lighting conditions.*

It seems to me that you factory farmers are far too fond of this 'simple and direct' strategy. Putting animals in unnatural and unpleasant environments produces unnatural and unpleasant behaviour. But, instead of ameliorating the environment even a smidgen – that would be unprofitable – you butcher the animals and make their environments even worse.

> *Yes, whatever. But why are you getting so upset? It's not as if the pig is going to be around for very long anyway.*

That is true. Roughly 20 weeks from the day it was welcomed into the world with a tooth, testicle and tail clipping, it will have reached a market weight of 100 kg (220 lb) and will be sent to slaughter.

Thank you, Mr Farmer. The short life of this pig is, of course, only part of a much bigger story. I have not, for example, broached the issue of where this pig came from. The life of a breeding sow is somewhat different from the

▲ A pig farm – the gross abuse of animal rights to gratify human demand for cheap pork products.

life described – and arguably worse! But the nightmarish lives typically led by the animals that humans like to eat is only the beginning. People often say to me things like this: 'Yes, I agree. The conditions these factory animals are raised in are unconscionable. That's why I only eat free-range animals, raised on family farms.' I agree with them that a world where the animals that humans eat have happy, healthy, more or less natural lives is a much, much better world, morally speaking, than the one we currently inhabit. Nevertheless, there is still the small matter of the animal's death. The death of the animals we eat will, typically, be at least as nightmarish as their lives. (If you doubt this, you might take a look at Eisnitz 2006 and Safran Foer 2009 – a strong stomach is required.) And, although some slaughterhouses are

> *'Auschwitz begins wherever someone looks at a slaughterhouse and thinks: they're only animals.'*

Theodor Adorno, German sociologist and philosopher

undoubtedly worse than others, there really is no such thing as a humane, free-range, family slaughterhouse, where animals happily gambol to their demise. But focusing on the horrific ways in which these animals die might lead us to overlook one further, rather important, consideration. They die. Remaining alive, rather than having one's life prematurely ended, is a vital interest of animals, just as it is a vital interest of humans. Not being killed is among the most vital interests anyone can ever have. It is laughable to suppose that when we raise and kill animals for food we are not sacrificing some of their most vital interests: because of the way they live, the way they die, and the fact that they die. If eating animals does not promote any similarly vital interests of humans, we have to conclude that it is morally wrong. This brings us to the second stand of the case against eating animals.

▶ So why eat meat?

Eating animals does not promote vital human interests. In fact, it does quite the opposite. Eating animals is so very bad for humans in so many (sometimes surprising) ways that, on any reasonable interpretation of the evidence, I think we have to conclude that the practice of eating meat is actually incompatible with many vital human interests.

There is a reason for eating meat. It tastes good. Some people deny this, but I am not going to contest it. Personally, I miss eating meat, especially during barbecue season when wonderful aromas regularly assault me from all sides and I can do little about it (and in Miami it's always barbecue season). Gustatory pleasure is a reason – and it's not, in itself, a bad one: pleasure provides a reason to do something. But it is not as if my life has been utterly ruined by a reduction in such pleasures – assuming there has even been a reduction. (Non-meat dishes can also taste good, maybe as good as their fleshy counterparts – although gustatory pleasure is, I suppose, in the mouth of the chewer.) Pleasures of the palate, in other words, hardly correspond to vital interests.

However, one might think that there are other reasons for eating meat, reasons other than gustatory pleasure. One possible reason might be that it is good for our health. We need protein – getting enough of that is a vital interest of ours. However, this argument works only if we assume that eating meat is the only way of getting the protein we need. That assumption is false. No one really knows how many vegetarians there are in the world. But the numbers are certainly huge. In India, for example, according to a survey jointly conducted in 2006 by *The Hindu* newspaper and CNN, the number of pure vegetarians is estimated to be 31 per cent of the 1.2 billion population – with a further 9 per cent of the population comprising vegetarians who eat eggs. In the US, a Gallup poll conducted in July 2012 found that around 7 per cent of the 311 million population identify themselves as either vegetarian or vegan. In the UK, various studies estimate between 3 and 11 per cent of the population are entirely vegetarian. According to the Italian research institute Eurispes, Italy has more than 6 million vegetarians, and the Institut Produkt and Markt arrives at a figure of more than 7 million Germans. Even if one decides to take these figures with some caution, one fact is clear: there are hundreds of millions of healthy vegetarians worldwide. Eating meat is clearly not required for health reasons. This is why the American Dietetic Association (ADA), the US's premier group of food and nutrition professionals, say things like this: 'Well-planned vegetarian diets are appropriate for all individuals during all stages of the life cycle, including pregnancy, lactation, infancy, childhood, and adolescence, and for athletes' (American Dietetic Association 2009).

In fact, as far as health considerations go, a well-planned vegetarian diet is almost certainly healthier than a meat-based diet. The problem is that with the protein that meat supplies come other things, things one could really do without – notably, saturated fat and cholesterol. Here, again, is the ADA:

> Vegetarian diets are often associated with a number of health advantages, including lower blood cholesterol levels, lower risk of heart-disease,

lower blood pressure levels, and lower risk of hypertension and type-2 diabetes. Vegetarians tend to have a lower body mass index (BMI) and lower overall cancer rates. (ibid.)

When you consider that heart disease and cancer together account for almost 50 per cent of the annual deaths in the US, the message seems unequivocal: good health is not a reason for eating meat; it is a reason for not eating meat. Indeed, the most commonly cited reason cited for conversion to a vegetarian diet is health.

◗ The meat industry and human health

There are other health risks associated with the animal industry. Almost everyone reading this book has been fortunate enough to be born in the age of antibiotics. Few remember what life was like before. I am told it was rather grim – in the tens-or-hundreds-of-millions-of-annual-deaths-from-now-easily-treatable-illnesses sense of grim.

That age looks as if it might be coming to an end. More and more bacteria are becoming antibiotic resistant. One of the more important reasons for this is the widespread use of antibiotics in the factory farming industry. Because of the appalling conditions in which they are raised, animals are susceptible to bacterial infections. Factory farmers pre-empt this by the widespread use of antibiotics in the animals' feed – whether the animals are sick or not. In the US, 8 million kg

(17.8 million lb) of antibiotics are given to animals each year, compared to around 1.4 million kg (3 million lb) given to humans (Grady 2001). And that is an industry claim – other estimates are higher. For example, the Union of Concerned Scientists puts the figure at 11.2 million kg (24.6 million lb) (UCS 2004). The problem is that these antibiotics are excreted, find their way into the soil and water, and there encounter microbes that will then have the opportunity to develop resistance to them.

Here's a little irony. As a father of two young children, I know that they have to be near death before their paediatrician will prescribe antibiotics to them. This is the result of an American Paediatric Association (APA) directive that discourages prescription of antibiotics except in cases of clear and overriding need. The rationale for this directive is increasing bacterial antibiotic resistance. Failing to complete a course of antibiotics can help promote antibiotic resistance. Therefore, reasons the APA, the fewer courses of antibiotics prescribed, the fewer courses will be uncompleted. Brilliant! Except, of course for the fact that nearly six times as many antibiotics are being fed to animals as to humans. My children can't get antibiotics unless they can demonstrate clear and significant suffering. The animals we eat get them just in case they become ill (which they will). If the age of antibiotics is, indeed, coming to an end, this has been significantly hastened by factory farming practices – another health cost of the animal industry. This is not new information. The consequences of non-therapeutic use of antibiotics in livestock have been understood for decades: scientists have been issuing warnings about it since the

1960s (HSUS 2007). These warnings have not been heeded because the power of the animal and pharmaceutical industries far exceeds that of medical professionals.

There are other possible implications for human health, or lack thereof. The 1918 Spanish flu pandemic killed somewhere between 50 and 100 million people. The virus that caused it has recently been discovered to be a mutated form of avian flu (Tauberberger et al. 2005). The H5N1 strain – 'bird flu' – originated in poultry. The World Health Organization (WHO) calculates, at a 'relatively conservative estimate', between 2 and 7.4 million deaths if the virus should become airborne. This is, of course, what happened to the H1N1 strain – swine flu – which is generally thought to have originated at the Smithfield factory pig farm in La Gloria, Mexico. The WHO cheerfully claims that 'the world may be on the brink of another pandemic' (WHO 2005). Breeding animals in large numbers in close proximity to each other provides fertile soil for the development and transmission of novel strains of viruses. Throw in a few humans, and conditions are ripe for mutation and cross-species transmission. It is difficult to see what would have to happen before we sit up and take notice. Pigs developing Ebola and passing it on to humans? Oh, wait, that's already happened (Racaniello 2005).

▶ Animals and the environment

The environmental costs of the animal industry are also staggering. A study by the Pew Commission, commissioned by the United Nations, demonstrated conclusively that, globally, farmed animals contribute more to climate change emissions than transport. That's all transport. The animal industry contributes 18 per cent of greenhouse-gas emissions, around 40 per cent more than the entire transport sector – ships, planes, trains and automobiles combined (FAO 2006a). Animal agriculture is responsible for 37 per cent of anthropogenic methane, which is 23 times more powerful in trapping UV light than CO_2, as well as 65 per cent of anthropogenic nitrous oxide, which has a monumental 298 times the global warming potential of CO_2. According to a University of Chicago study, the difference between a vegetarian and a meat-based diet is equivalent, in climate emission terms, to that between owning a mid-sized sedan and a large sport utility vehicle – just the news Hummer-driving vegetarians have been waiting for (Eshel & Martin 2006).

Disputes over water are predicted to become one of the leading causes of geopolitical unrest in this present century. It is not difficult to see the leading cause. It is well known that animal agriculture makes astonishing demands on water. It takes anywhere between 400 gallons (1,800 litres) and 2,400 gallons (11,000 litres) (depending on the animal – beef, for example, is far more water intensive than chicken) of water to produce one pound (0.45kg) of meat. This compares rather unfavourably to the 25 gallons (114 litres) of water it takes to produce one pound of wheat. Thus, John Anthony Allan, professor at King's College London, and winner of the prestigious Stockholm Water Prize, has argued that people worldwide should become vegetarian because of the tremendous waste of water involved in eating animals.

According to the US Environmental Protection Agency (EPA), run-off from factory farms pollutes more waterways than all other industries combined. Much of this run-off consists of excrement. The US animal agriculture industry produces roughly 39,463 kg (87,000 lb) of excrement per second – yes, *per second* (cited in Safran Foer 2009: 174). Not only does this far exceed the amount of excrement produced by the human population but there is, in addition, no waste-processing infrastructure in place to mitigate the animals' efforts. This run-off eventually reaches the sea where it causes, among other things, acidification and algal blooms. Australia's Great Barrier Reef has lost roughly half of its coral since 1985 – a pattern more or less replicated by coral reefs around the world. The two main causes are coral bleaching due to ocean warming (see the above remarks on climate emissions) and the coral-eating activities of the crown-of-thorns starfish, whose numbers have dramatically increased due to the increase in algal blooms (on which its larvae feed) caused by agricultural run-off.

The agricultural run-off in question is not, necessarily, from the animal industry. However, the distinction between animal and non-animal farming is increasingly becoming tenuous. Almost 40 per cent of the Earth's landmass is taken up by the growing of crops. And 70 per cent of those crops are now grown to feed animals (FAO 2006b). This is because of the grain–meat conversion ratio of roughly 16:1. That is, it takes up to 16 kg (35.3 lb) of grain to produce 1 kg (2.2 lb) of meat. In the US, for example, around 70 per cent of the grain and cereals grown is used to feed animals and not humans. The same is increasingly true in other countries. According to Greenpeace, roughly 1.2 million ha (2.9 million acres) of rainforest were destroyed in 2004–5 in order to grow crops – chiefly soy – that were used to feed chickens and other intensively raised animals. The destruction of rainforests is, of course, one of the more important contributors to climate change. And we have travelled full circle.

Eating animals violates their most vital interests without promoting any similarly vital human interests. Therefore it is morally wrong. Rather than promoting vital human interests, it actually jeopardizes some of the most vital human interests imaginable – interests in having a healthy body and a healthy environment. Therefore, it is terminally stupid. Both morally wrong and terminally stupid: it is difficult to imagine a more convincing case. Strangely, for a person who is optimistic about almost nothing, I am reasonably confident that the practice of eating meat, maybe not in my lifetime but not too long thereafter, will be consigned to the dustbin of history. Perhaps *in vitro* meat will provide a useful replacement or, at least, a weaning tool. Perhaps not. In any case, we will outgrow eating meat not because we will suddenly become more moral, or more intelligent, but because eventually we will be forced to accept that we have no choice. Eating meat is both a moral and a prudential disaster. We will outgrow it because we have to.

5

The mouse is a good place to start

'...research done on animals is frequently unreliable, misleading and contradictory. It cannot be trusted.'

The case against eating animals is compelling. Even if we overlook the dire effects the practice has on human health and the world we inhabit, eating animals overrides the most vital interests of animals for the sake of relatively trivial human ones. Therefore, eating animals treats them as if they do not count, morally speaking. But they do count. Therefore, eating animals is morally wrong. The practice of animal experimentation, however, might appear to have more respectable moral credentials. Some animal testing is done for medical research, and the focus of this is, it seems, life and health. These are clearly vital human interests. Therefore, this research cannot be condemned on the grounds that it allows the trivial interests of humans to trump the vital interests of animals. The moral case against eating animals, therefore, does not seem to extend to the practice of experimenting on them.

Others see the moral case against animal research very differently, arguing that animals have rights that should not be overridden, no matter how much benefit might accrue to human beings as a result. The idea of animal rights is, however, controversial, and in this book I am trying to work with a far more widely accepted idea: animals count, morally speaking – even if they don't count as much as humans. Given that this is the raw material I have to work with, my moral case extends no further than the claim that we should not sacrifice the vital interest of animals to further our own non-vital counterparts. So, while the case against eating animals is a strong one, the case against animal research seems far less so.

> *'Atrocities are not less atrocities when they occur in laboratories and are called medical research.'*

George Bernard Shaw, Irish playwright and political activist

However, matters are not as clear as they may seem. There are two questions that we need to consider. First, does research performed on animals even attempt to promote vital human interests? Some research clearly does, but not all. For example, testing of cosmetic products on animals is, despite some local prohibitions, still widespread, but does not serve any vital human interests. Moreover – and this is one of the most common forms of animal testing – new household products will be tested on animals to see whether they are carcinogens (cause cancer) or teratogens (cause birth defects). Avoiding cancer and not giving birth to horribly deformed babies are, of course, vital human interests. However, this does not mean that the animal research that is done for these reasons promotes vital human interests. For this to be true, the new product tested would have to be required to promote vital human interests (and not, for example, the economic interests of the developing company). If, for example, we didn't really need yet another option for cleaning our oven, or making our hair shiny and lustrous, any tests performed on animals to establish their safety does not, in fact, serve any vital human interest.

No one really knows the ratio of research that aims at promoting vital human interests to research that does not. There are several reasons for this. The first is a matter of bookkeeping. In the US, where the volume of animal testing dwarfs that in most other countries, there is no legal requirement to keep records of rodents used in experiments. Rodents are the animals most commonly used in animal testing. Second, there is misinformation. Tests for carcinogenicity and teratogenicity are often classified as vital research and overlook the issue of the status of the product tested.

Whatever the correct ratio is, it translates into huge numbers of animals. The British Union for the Abolition of Vivisection (BUAV) estimates that 100 million vertebrates are used in experiments annually. The Nuffield Council on Bioethics's estimation is between 50 and 100 million annually (NCB 2005). The United States Department of Agriculture (USDA) estimates that, excluding rodents, 1.17 million vertebrate animals were employed in experiments in 2005, 84,000 of which were subjected to pain without pain relief (APHIS 2005). The European Union employed 12 million animals in research experiments in 2005 (EFPIA 2011). Almost all experimental animals are euthanized at the conclusion of the experiments.

There is little benefit in citing further numbers. Both sides of the debate agree that they are large. I am more concerned with principle. To the extent that these animals are sacrificed to test products that do not promote vital human interests, what we do to these animals is morally wrong. No one knows precisely how many animals this applies to. Even pro-animal research publications such as Animal Research for Life accept that no more than

60 per cent of these animals is used for medical purposes (EFPIA 2011). (Note that this figure is for the EU, where cosmetic testing has been banned in several countries. For countries like the US, where such testing still occurs, this percentage of non-medical testing will inevitably be much higher.) Even if this figure is correct, it translates into millions and millions of animals whose suffering promotes no vital human interest. Such research is morally illegitimate and should not be performed.

▶ Vital research?

Let us now focus on research that does attempt to promote vital human interests: research conducted in the 'War on Cancer', heart disease, AIDS, and other life-threatening or -truncating human illnesses. Are these forms of research morally legitimate? The answer depends on how effective they are at promoting these interests. It is one thing to try to promote human vital interests, but if the methods one employs do not work, then they should not be adopted, no matter how laudable the goal. I think that, on any reasonable interpretation of the evidence, it is difficult to make a case for animal research being in general, effective in promoting vital human interests. This is not to say that animal research can never work, or that it has never played an important role in medical advances. The evidence does not support that claim either. Rather, the best interpretation of the evidence is that animal research is systematically unreliable, and can often be detrimental to vital human interests.

There is a clear moral and prudential case for replacing this research with more effective alternatives.

First, here are the basic facts: *92 per cent of drugs that pass pre-clinical testing, currently almost all* in vivo *animal-based, now fail clinical trials.* This figure is taken from the Food and Drug Administration's own *Critical Pathway* report (FDA 2004). The failure is due to the drug tested being either ineffective in humans or toxic to humans. Worse, if we exclude topical drugs (i.e. drugs applied to the skin) – for which the success rate is significantly higher – the failure rate is over 97 per cent. (Clearly, drugs aimed at the big killers like cancer and heart disease are not topical drugs.) Moreover, of the mere 8 per cent that do get approval based on animal trials, more than half of these will later be withdrawn or relabelled due to severe, unexpected side effects. Some defenders of animal testing take the attitude that this is just how it is with developing new medical products. We should expect high failure rates at each stage of testing. Interestingly, however, this was not the view of the FDA. Rather, in its *Critical Pathway* report, it concludes: 'Currently available animal models... have limited predictive value in many disease states.' Therefore, 'We must modernize the critical development path that leads from scientific discovery to the patient.' They also claim that animal toxicology is 'laborious, time-consuming, requires large quantities of product, and may fail to predict the specific safety problem that ultimately halts development'. It is not difficult to understand why animals are such poor models of human disease: there are crucial genetic, molecular, immunological and cellular differences between humans and other animals.

These basic facts and evaluations are supported by both historical examination and an analysis of practice today. First, let us look at history. How effective has animal testing been in the past?

'Practically all animal experiments are untenable on a statistical scientific basis, for they possess no scientific validity or reliability. They merely perform an alibi function for pharmaceutical companies, who hope to protect themselves thereby.'

Drs Margot and Herbert Stiller, founders of the German campaign group Ärzte gegen Tierversuche [Doctors against Animal Experimentation]

Consider, first, the connection between smoking and lung cancer. By 1963 studies on human patients had established a strong correlation. However, almost all experimental efforts to produce lung cancer in animals failed (Northrup 1957). Human and animal data disagreed, and this led to distrust of the human data. As a result, warnings were delayed for years and, arguably, many died as a result. This case is interesting in another respect. Today we are all too familiar with the way powerful lobbies work. Suppose there is a claim that is inimical to your interests but, the overwhelming preponderance of evidence suggests, is true. The way to deal with this is to find some 'experts' who are willing to side with you. Even if they are in a tiny majority, they can be used to cast doubt on the inconvenient claim. At the very least, this may delay for some time the implementation of action based on the claim. Just think, for example, of the strategy adopted by the oil and coal lobby to deal with the claim, overwhelmingly accepted among climate scientists, that current climate change has an anthropogenic origin. As we shall see, the results of animal research, being so inconsistent and conflicting, are ripe for this sort of exploitation. This can make the research positively harmful, as it was in the case of cigarettes and lung cancer.

In a similar vein, by the early 1940s, human clinical studies strongly suggested that asbestos causes cancer. However, animal trials repeatedly failed to demonstrate this, and, partly as a result, proper workplace precautions were not instituted until decades later (Enterline 1988).

It is tempting to marginalize the significance of history. Of course, we made mistakes back in those days, but surely we have pulled our act together now. This optimism, however, is difficult to sustain. In contemporary cancer research, the animal testing industry's animal of choice is the mouse. However, the industry's own *Lab Animal* magazine admits that 'mice are actually poor models of the majority of human cancers' (Lab Animal 2001). Leading cancer researcher Robert Weinberg writes: 'The preclinical [i.e. animal] models of human cancer, in large part, stink... Hundreds of millions of dollars are being wasted every year by drug companies using these models' (MRMC 2006). And another researcher, Clifton Leaf, himself a cancer survivor, comments: 'If you want to understand where the War on Cancer has gone wrong, the mouse is a pretty good place to start' (Leaf 2004). Richard Klausner, former Director of the National Cancer Institute, writes: 'The history of cancer research has been a history of curing cancer in the mouse. We have cured mice of cancer for decades, and it simply didn't work in humans' (cited *Los Angeles Times*, 6 May 1998).

Finally, even the *Handbook of Laboratory Animal Science* acknowledges the weakness of animal models of cancer. Commenting on a 25-year screening programme carried out by the National Cancer Institute, it states that:

> *40,000 plant species were tested for anti-tumour activity. Several of the plants proved effective and safe enough in the chosen animal model to justify clinical trials in humans. In the end, none of these drugs was found useful in therapy because of too high toxicity or ineffectivity in humans. This means that despite 25 years of intensive research and positive results in animal models, not a single anti-tumour drug emerged from this work.* (Hau, Svendsen and Schapiro 1994)

Following this failure of their screening programme, the National Cancer Institute (NCI) noted its 'dissatisfaction with the performance of prior *in vivo* primary screens [i.e. animal cancer tests]' (quoted in MRMC 2006: 7). As a result, they abandoned animal testing, replacing it with 59 human cancer cell lines to screen compounds for anti-cancer activity.

These failures are not unexpected. Tumours in animals often behave quite differently from human tumours, growing much more quickly and regressing spontaneously. They are also of different types: mice, for example, suffer from high rates of muscle and bone tumours, which are comparatively rare in humans. There are well-documented variations between species' responses to therapeutic drugs, grounded in significant metabolic differences (for more details, see MRMC 2006).

A similar picture emerges when we shift our focus from cancer to AIDS research. Animal studies have been extensively employed in this research but whether they have contributed any significant results is unclear. Mice, rabbits and monkeys – the animals most used in this research – can be infected with HIV, but rarely develop the AIDS syndrome. More than 150 chimpanzees have been infected with HIV since research began, but only one developed the AIDS syndrome (and even in this case the evidence is equivocal) (MRMC 2006: 4; O'Neill et al. 2000). Furthermore, there have been more than 100 human clinical trials conducted. Of the more than 50 preventive vaccines and more than 30 therapeutic vaccines that were successful in HIV in animal studies, none was successful in subsequent clinical studies MRMC 2006: 4). These failures contrast markedly with the success of human clinical investigation, which allowed researchers to isolate the HIV virus, to identify both the disease's natural course and its risk factors.

In vitro research using human white blood cells identified both the efficacy and toxicity of anti-AIDS medicines, including AZT, 3TC and protease inhibitors.

Toxicity testing is one of the most common types of animal research – in particular, testing for carcinogenicity (capacity to produce cancer) and teratogenicity (capacity to produce birth defects). Rodent studies for carcinogenicity have been estimated to yield a 95-per-cent rate of false positives. Lave et al., writing in the journal *Nature*, conclude: 'Tests for human carcinogens using lifetime rodent bioassays are expensive, time-consuming, and give uncertain results.' They conclude that rodent cancer studies are 'scientifically invalid' and 'fiscally indefensible' (Lave 1988).

As an example, one of many, consider the cases of two widely used artificial sweeteners: saccharin and aspartame. Saccharin produces bladder cancer in rats. However, this is only if you force the rat to ingest the equivalent of 1,100 cans of a diet beverage. And it only produces cancer in male rats. The reason is that they possess higher levels of a protein that interacts with saccharin to form crystals in the bladder. The protein is absent in humans (MRMC 2006: 12). Aspartame, on the other hand, is associated with an increased risk of lymphomas and leukaemias in rats. However, this is only true of female rats. And it does not seem to be true of humans. Epidemiological studies of 340,045 men and 226,945 women failed to show any increased cancer risk (Lim et al. 2006).

Because of the marked unreliability of animal testing, the NCI has long abandoned animal testing for carcinogenicity. The 59 human cell lines it established to test compounds for anti-cancer properties have been supplemented with another 100 human cell lines that it now uses to test products for carcinogenicity.

Animal testing for teratogenicity (abnormalities in physiological development) is, if anything, even more unreliable. Bailey et al. conducted a comprehensive review of animal tests of 1,396 substances. Of those substances known to cause birth defects in humans, animal tests indicated that almost half were safe. Conversely, of those substances known to be safe in humans, animal tests indicated that almost half were dangerous. Moreover, almost one-third of all substances tested yielded varying results depending on the species chosen (Bailey et al. 2005).

Of course, there are examples of medical research where testing on animals seems to have played a more beneficial role. However, even here, the value of this role is not unambiguous. The development of the polio vaccine is often cited as a paradigm example of the benefits of animal research. It is true that monkey cell cultures were used for vaccine production. However, it was research with human cell cultures that first demonstrated that the poliovirus could be grown on non-neural tissue. Moreover, animal models resulted in a misunderstanding of the mechanism of infection – suggesting transmission by the respiratory rather than the digestive route. This misdirected preventive measures and delayed the development of tissue-culture methodologies critical to the discovery of a vaccine (MRMC 2006: 2).

▶ The alternatives

These examples merely scratch the surface of the shortcomings of animal research. The evidence is not enough to show that animal studies can never be useful in medical research – after all, how would one prove a negative? But I think it is enough to show that research done on animals is frequently unreliable, misleading and contradictory. It cannot be trusted. If there are alternatives, we should pursue them with enthusiasm. There are available alternatives, and these are improving by the day (MRMC 2006: 14ff.). The relevance of these alternatives will depend on the type of medical research being conducted.

First, there is *epidemiology*. For example, human population studies identified the major risk factors for coronary disease (smoking, elevated cholesterol, high blood pressure). These studies also showed that smoking triples age-specific mortality rates; that giving up by the age of 50 halves the risk; and that giving up by the age of 30 eliminates the risk almost entirely.

Second, there are *studies on individual patients*. For example, the claim that a low-fat vegetarian diet, regular exercise, smoking cessation and stress management techniques could reverse heart disease was initially established through close monitoring of individual patients. Modern, non-invasive imaging devices such as CAT, MRI, PET and SPECT scans have now revolutionized clinical investigation.

Third, there are *autopsies and biopsies*. Autopsies have been an important tool in our understanding of many diseases – including heart disease, appendicitis, diabetes and Alzheimer's disease. The information provided by autopsies is, generally, restricted to the final stages of a disease, but biopsies can supply valuable information about a disease in other stages of development. For example, endoscopic biopsies demonstrated that colon cancer often develops from benign tumours called adenomas. (In contrast, colon cancer in a leading animal model appears to lack this adenoma-to-carcinoma sequence (Pories et al. 1993)). Small skin biopsies (where the capillaries remain intact) can be used to reveal the cardiovascular effects or risks of a new drug.

Fourth, there is *post-marketing surveillance*. Advances in computer techniques permit detailed and comprehensive records of drug side effects, allowing identification of both the dangers and beneficial side effects of new drugs. For example, the anti-cancer properties of prednisone, nitrogen mustard and Actinomycin D were discovered in this way. So, too, were the tranquillizing effect of chlorpromazine and the mood-elevating effect of MAO-inhibitors and tricyclic antidepressants (MRMC 2006: 17).

Fifth, there are *in vitro studies* that have proved to be powerful investigative tools. The NCI now has 60 human cancer cell lines to test chemotherapeutic drugs, and does not use animal assays. Similarly, *in vitro* tests with human DNA can detect DNA damage much more readily than animal studies. On general grounds of reliability of results, some pharmaceutical companies – for example, Biopta and Asterand – have abandoned animal studies and now work exclusively with human tissue.

Sixth, there are *microfluidic organ chips*. The limitations of tissue cultures are well known. Bodies are made up of different organs/systems, and how a drug acts will often be dependent on how it has been processed by these organs. Its properties might differ substantially, for example, before and after its processing by the liver. A promising way of circumventing these limitations is by way of multiple, connected organ chips. Microfluidic circuits comprise nodes, containing cells from various human organs, linked by a circulating blood substitute. This allows the drug to encounter cells in the order in which it would encounter them in the human body.

Seventh, there is *computer modelling*. Growing more sophisticated by the day, this technique allows drugs to be designed on computers and then tested on virtual organs or in virtual clinical trials – making it possible to simulate in hours experiments that would take months or years to perform on animals. There is, for example, Bayer's PK-SIM™, which conducts whole-body simulations, from absorption to distribution, metabolism

▲ Is it really possible to justify animal suffering on the grounds of improbable medical advances?

and excretion. Obviously, computer modelling can be combined with microfluidic systems.

Finally, there is *micro-dosing*. Human micro-dosing involves the introduction of minuscule doses of a drug (typically around 1 per cent of the normal dose) in order to evaluate drug activity in a human body. This evaluation is carried out through the use of extraordinarily sensitive analytical techniques. The technique has proved quite accurate, with the results of micro-dosing studies showing a 70-per-cent correspondence with those from full-dose studies – a vast improvement over animal models. Both the FDA and the European Agency for the Evaluation of Medicinal Products have endorsed its use, and it may well eventually replace unreliable animal testing as part of the first phase of pre-clinical testing for every drug.

Animal experimentation is a subject on which reasonable disagreement is possible. Ironically, every effort seems to have been made to ensure that the disagreement is anything but that. But here, I think, are two claims that cannot be denied. First, much research on animals does not even aim at promoting vital human interests. This research, because it violates the vital interests of animals, is morally wrong. Second, of the research performed on animals that does aim at promoting vital human interests – primarily medical research – much of it is useless. In fact, the numbers suggest – if we add together both the drugs that fail clinical testing and those later withdrawn because of unforeseen side effects – a failure rate of over 95 per cent. If we exclude topical medicines, that failure rate is not too far off 99 per cent. Opposition to animal testing is often portrayed as anti-science. But it can hardly be anti-science to question a process that is so farcically inefficient.

Research using animals is sometimes portrayed as absolutely essential to human health. I was once in a public debate with a researcher who claimed, with no suggestion of humour, that without animal experimentation the human race would have become extinct by now. This claim is, of course, inane. Even if we confine the category of 'human' to modern humans (based on anatomical rather than behavioural modernity), humans have been around for 200,000 years. In contrast, animal experimentation has been with us for a few hundred years or so, and been extensively practised for a little more than 100 of those years. We were, apparently, doing rather well before the development of modern medical science.

Moreover, arguably the single biggest contribution to human health was not the development of medical science but the development of *plumbing*. As a result, the big killer diseases of the preceding centuries – typhoid, cholera, plague – were already in steep decline when animal experimentation was in its infancy, and this decline was largely complete before the practice of animal testing became widespread. More recently, the decline in lung cancer has consistently tracked the decline in the numbers of smokers. A similar decline in heart disease and cancer would almost certainly result if more people ate healthier diets and exercised consistently.

On the other hand, the claim that animal experimentation can never foster medical progress is also probably false. If research on animals can effectively promote vital human interests, and if there is no other way of achieving the same result (*in vitro*, microfluidic systems, computer modelling, micro-dosing, etc.), then no argument developed in this book can count against it. (Other arguments, of course, may. I shall not pursue those arguments here. For some of the more influential arguments, see Garrett 2012, and for my 'two-penn'orth', Rowlands 2002: Chapter 7.) I think that the preponderance of the available evidence strongly suggests that, at best, only a small amount of research performed on animals meets these conditions – although let us accept that some does. The conclusion, therefore, seems to be that most research conducted on animals is immoral. Alternatives to this research should, therefore, be pursued, for both moral and prudential reasons.

6

A house made of gingerbread

'If we overlook the terror and pain inflicted by some hunting practices, the most obvious vital interest violated by hunting is the interest in staying alive.'

Hunting animals can be done for at least three reasons: food, pest control and sport. I will discuss hunting for sport in the next chapter. This chapter discusses hunting that is done for food or to control the numbers of certain sorts of animals. The framework within which this discussion takes place is, by now, a familiar one. First, does hunting take priority over the vital interests of the animals hunted? Second, if it does, are there any similarly vital human interests that hunting promotes? If the answer to both these questions is 'no', then hunting is morally wrong. I shall argue that the answers to both these questions are – not always, but almost always – 'no'.

▶ Staying alive

When animals are raised for food, or experimented upon, they typically lead lives that range from the merely miserable to the utterly nightmarish. This is not the case for the animals targeted by hunters. Their lives are lived in the wild and, while they may be hard and short, they are not the nightmarish existences of the factory pig or the cancer mouse. If we overlook the terror and pain inflicted by some hunting practices, the most obvious vital interest violated by hunting is the interest in staying alive. Some people think that animals have no such interest. An interest in staying alive is equivalent to an interest in not dying. In order to have this latter interest, you need to understand what death is. Animals don't understand what death is. Therefore, they don't have an interest in staying alive.

The premise of the argument might be correct. To understand what death is you have to understand that it is irrevocable. Nevermore will you walk on the earth and feel the sun on your face, and so on. To have the concept of death you must have the concept of nevermore – and it is far from clear that animals can have this concept. Nevertheless, the argument is unconvincing. If we were to accept it, we would also have to accept that babies and young children have no interest in staying alive – because they don't understand what death is, either. Does it follow that they have no interest in staying alive? If so, in killing them painlessly we violate no interest of theirs. This claim is stunningly implausible. Where has the argument gone wrong?

A baby has no idea what death is – and, therefore, no idea what life is. If it does not have the concept of life, how can it have an interest in staying alive? The answer, of course, is that staying alive is a precondition of the satisfaction of all its other interests. Being a baby, its explicit interests are rather limited: warmth, milk, etc. But if it dies, none of these interests will be satisfied. Therefore, the baby does have an interest in staying alive, even if it has no concept of life or death. This is the sense in which a creature can have an interest in staying alive, even if it does not understand what death is. Animals and young children that cannot understand death can still have an interest in staying alive because satisfying this interest is a precondition of satisfying any interest. As such, the interest in staying alive is about as vital an interest as it is possible to have. When we kill an animal, we put an end to all of its interests, and this is why killing it is a violation of one of its most vital interests imaginable.

▶ Hunting for food

Hunting, therefore, clearly does violate a vital interest of animals. The question, now, is whether it also promotes similarly vital human interests. Consider, first, the case of hunting for food. In certain circumstances, of course, hunting for food might indeed promote the vital interests of the human hunters. If there were no other food around, for example, or very little food, then hunting animals would promote vital human interests and there could be no moral objection to it. Therefore, in the case of certain human societies living on the margins of existence – the Inuit provide an obvious example – there is no moral objection to hunting animals for food.

While some hunting for food is morally legitimate, it is pretty clear that most is not. Most hunting for food – certainly most hunting carried out in developed nations – does not meet the required conditions of promoting vital human interests. Most hunting for food is carried out in places where there are plenty of other food sources available, most of which can be accessed more easily (and often more cheaply) than the animals hunted. Therefore, in the vast majority of cases, hunting animals for food is not morally legitimate.

Sometimes it is claimed that hunting is actually good for the animals. For example, if we didn't shoot a certain number of deer each year, their numbers would soon explode. Overgrazing would result, yielding environmental degradation and a slow, painful death for many of the deer. A quick death via the huntsman's bullet is better than a slow death from starvation. True, it is unfortunate for the animals that actually get killed – their vital interests are overridden. But the vital interests of many more animals are actually promoted. So, you see, hunting animals is actually in their best interests: it promotes the vital interests of the group, even if it sacrifices the interests of some of the individuals.

There are, I think, many problems with this argument. First of all, death by a huntsman's bullet is often far from quick and painless: shocking as it may sound, there are many hunters who don't shoot very well at all, even when sober. (When I lived in Alabama, the one place you absolutely, positively did not want to find yourself was in the country on the first day of the hunting season.) Even if we overlook this problem, the argument still faces insurmountable difficulties. First of all, game management strategies generally operate on the principle of maximum sustainable yield. Shoot only as many deer in each year as will allow the maximum number to be shot the following year. In other words, the goal of game management strategies is to ensure that the maximum number of animals can be killed over time. These strategies have nothing to do with protecting either the group or the environment. The environment is an afterthought, and the group is relevant only to the extent that it supplies the maximum number of animals for slaughter.

Perhaps this is irrelevant. Even if protection of the group or the environment is not the goal of game management strategies, maybe they are protected anyway – an unintended but fortuitous consequence of those strategies. This, I think, brings us to the crux of the matter. Why is it, for example, that deer numbers would explode if humans didn't regularly head to the woods and blast away at them? The answer is that some natural keystone predator has been eradicated. In the US and much of Europe, that predator was the wolf. And why was this predator eradicated? Typically, it was because people who hunted deer and animals of that ilk wanted more deer to shoot. Kill the wolves, so you can shoot more deer – and then bleat on about protecting the environment. It's rather cynical.

OK, one might think. But what difference does it make whether it is we who are killing the deer with our guns or wolves killing them with their teeth? It's all the same to the deer, surely? In fact, if I were a deer, I think I would prefer the rifle, assuming the person behind it is a remotely good shot. This is a good question, but proper discussion will have to be postponed until the discussion of predation in a later chapter. The short answer is that morality is not simply about pain and pleasure. It's about doing what is right and not doing what is wrong. That is, it is about trying to maximize the number of things that are right in the world and minimizing the number of things that are wrong. When a wolf eats a deer, it has no choice: it eats or dies. It is not doing anything wrong. We do have a choice – we can eat things that do not suffer. If we eat things that suffer, we are doing something wrong. However, while we should, morally speaking, try to eliminate certain things we do, there is no corresponding moral obligation to eliminate what the wolf does.

▶ Pest control

The subject of wolves brings us to the second type of hunting: pest control. For much of human history, wolves have been regarded as pests or vermin – and that's how they are still viewed in large swathes of the world. The term 'pest' is, of course, a loaded one, and the first thing to consider is how some animals came to be recipients of this label. 'Pest' basically denotes a competitor. An animal is a pest when it competes with humans in some way – when its interests and ours conflict. Thus, wolves are 'pests' because they eat deer, elk and livestock. Foxes are 'pests' because they eat lambs and chickens. In eradicating these pests, one might argue, we are, in fact, protecting animals. This claim, however, takes the cynicism we found in the environmental argument for hunting and elevates it to an entirely new level. If protection from being eaten is involved at all, it doesn't extend very far. We are protecting animals from being eaten only so that we can eat them ourselves.

'Heaven is by favor; if it were by merit your dog would go in and you would stay out. Of all the creatures ever made [man] is the most detestable. Of the entire brood, he is the only one

> *[...] that possesses malice. He is the only creature that inflicts pain for sport, knowing it to be pain.'*
>
> *Mark Twain, American writer*

Suppose you live in a gingerbread house and have a marked predilection for cannibalism. You regularly slaughter the large predators living in the

▲ The hunting of wolves in countries such as Sweden and the United States offers a particularly dramatic example of the hypocrisy of 'culling', often supposedly carried out in the interests of other species or the environment, but usually enjoyed by humans as thinly disguised bloodlust.

forest – wolves, lynx and bear – in which your gingerbread house is situated, to keep the local village children safe. But this is only because you want to lure them to your gingerbread residence and make them into pies. That is pretty much the sort of protection we offer animals when we rid the world of 'pests'.

Consider, as an example, the hunting of wolves as carried out in the US, an activity that resulted in their virtual extinction in the 48 contiguous states. After extensive Federal efforts to reintroduce them to their native range, wolves started making the beginnings of a comeback. However, several states – Montana, Idaho and Wyoming – have succeeded in having wolves delisted from the Endangered Species Act (even though they are manifestly still endangered), and run regular wolf 'culls' – whittling down the wolf numbers in those states to, once again, near zero. The purpose of these culls is to 'protect' livestock, deer and elk. Of course, the purpose of this 'protection' is to keep those animals alive long enough for humans to eat them or shoot them, or both. Since shooting these animals to eat them is wrong – because it sacrifices the vital interests of animals without promoting any similarly vital human interests – we cannot appeal to these practices to justify the extermination of wolves. That would be like the witch appealing to her practice of eating children to justify her killing of the forest's large predators. You cannot, in other words, justify actions by appealing to morally bankrupt practices.

Consider, as another example, foxhunting as it was practised, until recently, in the UK. Foxes are pests. Therefore, we should saddle up some horses, release some appropriately trained dogs, and chase the foxes around the countryside until we can kill them. If we don't do this, their numbers will explode (again, this is because we have exterminated the larger predators). Even if we overlook certain factual problems – for example, numerous studies have shown that hunting foxes with hounds seems to make very little difference to fox numbers – there is a fundamental moral problem with the argument. Foxes are pests only because they eat the animals we want to eat, or eat animals whose products we want to eat. To justify the slaughter of foxes by appealing to a practice that is morally illegitimate is, once again, not going to work. I refer you to the case of the witch and her house of gingerbread.

To summarize: hunting always involves the sacrifice of the vital interests of the animals hunted. It almost always fails to promote similarly vital human interests. There are no other considerations that could justify hunting. Therefore, hunting is, almost always, morally wrong.

7

It's not so much bullfighting...

'The difference between blood and non-blood sports is, to some extent, a matter of degree rather than kind.'

A third category of hunting – sports hunting – is really part of another type of activity in which animals can engage (or, more commonly, be made to engage): sports. In assessing the moral status of sports involving animals, we must again look to our two guiding questions. First, are the vital interests of animals being upheld by the sport? Second, are any similarly vital interests of humans being promoted by the sport? If the answer to both questions is 'no', then the sport is morally wrong. However, whether this is the answer to both questions will almost certainly vary from sport to sport. There is, I shall argue, no blanket answer to the question of whether sports involving animals are right or wrong.

Sports involving animals can be divided into two sorts. First, there are blood sports: sports where the death or injury of the animals involved is either an explicit goal of the sport or an almost inevitable consequence of it. Bullfighting, for example, aims at, and almost always leads to, the death of the bull. Dogfighting sometimes involves the death of one of the dogs involved in the fight, and injury to at least one dog is an almost inevitable consequence of it. Both activities, therefore, count as blood sports.

Non-blood sports are sports that involve animals but do not aim at their death or injury. Neither is death or injury a likely consequence of the sport – although it may occasionally occur as a consequence. For example, some types of horse races – steeplechases such as the English Grand National are a good example – involve jumping over fences so large that some horses will fall, sustain injury, and either die immediately or subsequently be destroyed. The difference between blood and non-blood sports is, to some extent, a matter of degree rather than kind. Whether the Grand National counts as a blood sport depends on the frequency with which horses perish when running it. Once a certain threshold is met – and it is far for clear where, exactly, that threshold is – the race would have to be regarded as a blood sport.

▶ Sport and spectacle

Consider, first, blood sports. In such sports, the vital interests of the animals are clearly being sacrificed: the animals die or are seriously injured. Do these sports promote any corresponding vital interests of humans? If so, what would those interests be?

Spectacle – being entertained – is not a vital interest of humans. And even if it were, there are plenty of other spectacles around that do not involve inflicting death or injury on animals. Go and watch a football game, or a performance of *Les Misérables*, for example. Sometimes there is an appeal to tradition: the sport in question has been practised/loved by our fathers and their fathers before them, and now forms part of the rich cultural fabric of society, and should be protected on these grounds. The problem, however, is that appeals to tradition only work if the tradition in question is not seriously morally wrong. Slavery, for example, is a traditional way of life: almost all civilizations have at some point engaged in it. Few, I assume, would be willing to defend slavery by appeal to tradition. The appeal would not work for the simple reason that slavery is wrong. Moral reasons trump appeal to tradition.

Consider a tradition involving animals: *blood festivals*, of which bullfighting is the most familiar. These festivals can actually take various forms. A well-known one takes place in the Spanish town of Tordesillas each year. It's called the Toro de la Vega and involves thousands of men chasing a bull through the streets, beating it with sticks, pelting it with stones, and stabbing it with spears. When the bull is exhausted, its ears and testicles are sliced off – the man who finally kills the bull has the 'honour' of carrying these around the town on a spear. Defenders of the festival claim that it is part of the rich cultural heritage of Spanish life – and the taxes of citizens from all over the EU are used to subsidize this and many other festivals like it. The appeal to tradition, in this case, would work only if the Toro de la Vega were not morally wrong. To appeal to tradition, therefore, is to assume that the festival is not wrong – which is precisely the question at issue. The appeal to tradition is, therefore, question begging, in the sense that it assumes the claim that it is supposed to establish (i.e. that the practice is morally legitimate).

The same problem afflicts the attempt to justify blood sports on aesthetic grounds. You often find this attempt made to justify bullfighting. Here, for example, is one of the practice's apologists, Alexander Fiske-Harrison: 'There's something tragic about a bullfight. It's like a piece of theatre – it's even in three acts – and I think it is its artistic quality which mitigates and justifies the undeniable suffering the bull undergoes in the ring'

(Fiske-Harrison 2011: 73–4). So let us accept, for the sake of argument, that bullfighting is art. Ever since Marcel Duchamp attached a urinal to a wall and named it *Fountain*, the boundaries of art have been disputed. But whether or not bullfighting qualifies is irrelevant. The Costa Rican artist Guillermo Vargas once (reputedly – although what actually happened is a matter of dispute) starved a dog to death in a gallery in Nicaragua. He claimed this was art. Even if correct, this is no justification. The point is not that bullfighting is just like starving a dog to death. Rather it is that, if an activity is seriously morally wrong, then it should not be done even if it is art. Therefore, Fiske-Harrison's appeal to art will work only if we assume that bullfighting is not seriously morally wrong. In other words, his appeal to art is, like the appeal to tradition, question begging.

Sometimes it is argued that blood sports are justifiable on the grounds that they allow for the expression of certain important human virtues – courage being the one usually cited. The British philosopher Roger Scruton (1996) has defended foxhunting on these grounds. Many have defended bullfighting in this way. It is, of course, difficult to maintain that engaging in blood sports does involve this virtue at all – at least in the vast majority of blood sports. Maybe, if the animals shot at were armed with, and could operate, semi-automatic weapons, a case for sport hunting could be made on these grounds. The people who watch dogfights are not brave. Even in cases such as bullfighting, the role of courage is less than clear. Even if the matador is brave, the crowd baying him on is not. There are, even by conservative estimates, several hundred thousand bull deaths to every matador death, and so the mortal danger to the bullfighter on any given day is actually rather small. Given this disparity, we might conclude that, as Winston Churchill once was reputed to have said: 'It's not bullfighting, it's bull torture.' But, most importantly, even if blood sports do involve the virtue of courage, there are various other ways to develop and exercise that virtue without sacrificing the vital interests of animals: by jumping out of a plane, for example. Or, if you want a fight, get into the Octagon with a consenting human adult.

Blood sports sacrifice the vital interest of large numbers of animals. I haven't even broached the numbers of animals killed in training, which significantly outnumber the numbers actually killed in the sports themselves. For every bull that dies in the arena, many have died in the process of training the bullfighter. For every dog that fights in the pit, one or more dogs – strays or stolen pets – have died in the process of teaching that dog to kill. Blood sports sacrifice the most vital interests of animals, and do not serve to promote any similarly vital human interests – none that could plausibly be used to justify the practice. These sports are, therefore, morally wrong.

▶ Consenting participants?

Consider, now, non-blood sports. Some, perhaps persuaded by the animal rights agenda, argue that these, too, are morally illegitimate. To back this up, they might cite examples of such sports where death has resulted, even if it was not intended. The Grand National provides a steady stream of such examples. Furthermore, there are serious issues involving the welfare of the animals we use for these sports. For example, when their racing days are over, many greyhounds are simply killed or abandoned. These, admittedly, are awful abuses. But they are not essential to the sports themselves. One might reduce the size of the fences the horses have to jump, for example, or even eliminate fences altogether. One could enact legislation, and actually enforce it, to ameliorate the plight of greyhounds. While sports involving animals are ripe for abuse, this sort of abuse does not seem to be essential to the sports. And so they do not show that the sports themselves are morally illegitimate.

▲ A bullfight – the triumph of aesthetics over ethics?

Another common argument is that sports involving animals are wrong because animals cannot give their consent. As a general claim, this simply seems to be patently false, and people presumably make it because they think consent must be verbal or written. For example, many people run with their dogs. Running is a sport. Can dogs not give their consent? Suppose you say to your dog: 'Do you want to go for a run?' He or she starts bouncing around the room with excitement. I think it is pretty safe to take this as an expression of consent. My dog will behave in this way. Sometimes, in the Miami summer, upon walking out of the front door, he will decide it is too hot, sit down, and refuse to move. It is equally safe to take this as a withdrawal of consent to run.

Perhaps running with a dog is not what people have in mind by 'sport'. Maybe we should restrict the prohibition on animals in sport to competitive sports. But this is not plausible, either. Running with dogs can be a competitive sport. The sport is known as CaniX, and, apparently, it has its own world championship. The idea that dogs cannot give their consent to feature in these competitive events is, again, implausible. Or take another competitive sport involving dogs: Schutzhund – essentially martial arts for dogs involving, obedience, tracking and protection. In my experience, the dogs that engage in doing this not only don't mind what they are being asked to do but experience it as one of the high points of their lives.

Similarly, anyone who has ridden a horse, even in off-the-cuff racing events, would be very surprised to be told that the horses do not give their consent. Horses love to compete. Even a horse that spends most of its time lugging tourists around a beach becomes a completely different horse when allowed to compete with its fellow holiday workers in a barrel race.

In general, animals not only *can* give their consent to engage in sports; they frequently do give this consent. We know enough about many animals to know whether or not they are consenting – we just have to be honest. A sport involving an animal is, I think, morally legitimate as long as the following three conditions are met:

1 The animal consents to engage in the sport (and if more than one animal is involved, all must consent)

2 The sport does not aim at death or injury, and these are not probable consequences of engaging in the sport

3 There is sufficient legislation – in place and, crucially, enforced – to safeguard the welfare of animals that we engage in these sports.

In other words: as long as the animal consents, as long as the sport is not a blood sport, and as long as there is effective legislation that prevents likely abuses of animals involved in the sport, then sports involving animals are morally legitimate.

8

We'd better come up with a good name

'That a familial animal is of benefit to a human ... is no guarantee that the benefit runs both ways.'

What do we call them? 'Pet' is frowned on in some circles – a little un-PC, apparently. Perhaps more significantly, it's a bit of a stupid word. The alternative currently favoured by some, 'companion animals', seems a little forced to me. 'Familiars' sounds far too witchy, of course, but I'm going to go with a close variation, *familials*: familial animals – animals kept not (primarily) for profit but as members of the family, more or less. My Word spellcheck doesn't seem to like it, and it probably won't catch on anyway – none of my neologisms ever does. But whatever name we eventually select, it had better be a good one because there are a lot of them around – these creatures formerly known as pets. Indeed, in much of the developed world, their population edges slightly ahead of their human counterparts. In the UK, for example, there are, as of 2011, 63,181,775 humans (UK Census 2011). In 2012 the UK familial population was estimated to be around 67 million (PFMA 2012). As of the end of the Mayan calendar, the human population of the US was 314,979,793 (US Census Bureau 2012). At the same time, the estimated US familial population was around 357 million (PPA 2012).

Familials come in various forms. There are the traditional dog, cat and goldfish, and the equally traditional caged bird, hamster, mouse, gerbil and guinea pig. There is the slightly more edgy rat. There are snakes, lizards, newts, salamanders, frogs and toads. There are various species of non-caged fowl. There are horses and ponies. Increasingly, familials veer towards the exotic: lions, panthers, bobcats, wolves and wolf dogs. There are estimated to be around the same number of tigers in private hands in Texas as there are in the wild in Asia – a little more than 3,000 in each case.

The sheer variety of familial animals is indicative of some of the limitations of the term. The extent to which an animal is a familial is a matter of degree. A goldfish (and fish are by far the most numerous familials) that spends its life swimming around an aquarium does not seem to be a 'member of the family' to the same extent as the cat that spends its life curled up on its human's lap. The tiger that spends its life in a cage in Texas is, arguably, even less of a member of the family. The category of familials is, therefore, a relatively loose one. We might think of it as being fixed by way of certain paradigm cases of familials – the house dog and house cat being the most obvious – and others falling within the category to the extent that they resemble these paradigm cases. That is, the concept of a familial is a resemblance concept. An animal can be more or less a familial one. The greater its spatial proximity to the humans who care for it, and the more it is able to interact with them in ways that are natural to it, then the greater is the extent to which we will be inclined to regard it as a familial animal.

> 'Until you have loved an animal,
> part of your soul will have remained
> dormant.'
>
> *Anatole France, French writer*

A familial animal is also one that is not kept primarily for profit. The qualification 'primarily' is intended to allow for cases where, for example, the family dog is hired out for stud on an occasional basis while, at the same time, excluding the dogs of the notorious puppy mills. The latter are not familials; they are breeding machines (and the arguments against this practice are essentially the same as those against factory farming). The fact that familials are not kept primarily for profit has an important consequence. Familials cost money: purchase, upkeep, veterinary care and miscellaneous expenses. Despite the often significant costs, familials outnumber humans, at least in the parts of the world where people are most likely to be able to meet those costs. This suggests that the keeping of animals as familials meets some deep-seated human need. It is not entirely clear what that need is. Perhaps it is the need for companionship. Perhaps it is the need to spend at least some part of one's life with what is not human. Whatever the reason, to be in the presence of familial animals is a natural, and almost certainly beneficial, thing for humans. Among the documented benefits of (at least some) familials are: lower stress levels, decreased blood pressure, reduced cholesterol and triglycerides, improved mood and improved immune function. In short, familials tend to keep their humans alive for longer (CDC 2007).

▶ A mutually beneficial relation?

That a familial animal is of benefit to a human, however, is no guarantee that the benefit runs both ways. Human treatment of familials ranges from the good to the morally appalling. For example, in the US, between 6 and 8 million dogs and cats find their way into animal shelters each year. Between 3 and 4 million of them will be euthanized (ASPCA 2013). Because of the abuses to which familial animals are undoubtedly subject, many animal rights theorists have advocated the abolition of familial ownership, and this goes hand in hand with a persistent line of thought in animal rights circles: human interactions with animals are necessarily exploitative and, therefore, the only ethical stance we can have with regard to animals is to leave them alone. Here, for example, is the leading light in the 'leave them alone' wing, Gary Francione:

> *We ought not to bring any more domesticated nonhumans into existence. I apply this not only to animals we use for food, experiments, clothing, etc. but also to our non-human companions... We should certainly care for those nonhumans whom we have already brought into existence but we should stop causing any more to come into existence... it makes no sense to say that we have acted immorally in domesticating non-human animals but we are now committed to allowing them to continue to breed.* (Francione 2007)

So, that's it: no more familials. Because it was wrong to bring familials into existence in the first place, morality requires that we now ensure they die out. This argument is rather unconvincing. For example, it was clearly morally wrong to transport people from Africa to the Americas as slaves. Justice clearly requires the abolition of slavery. But that does not mean abolishing the existence of the former slaves. As Donaldson & Kymlicka (2011: 79) put it: 'Shipping slaves to America was certainly an injustice, but the remedy is not to seek the extinction of African Americans, or repatriate them to Africa.' The remedy, rather, was to put the relationship between the different races on an ethical footing. Therefore, our question is: What would an ethical relationship between humans and familials look like – at least in broad outline?

> *'I became a vegetarian after realizing that animals feel afraid, cold, hungry and unhappy like we do. I feel very deeply about vegetarianism and the animal kingdom. It was my dog Boycott who led me to question the right of humans to eat other sentient beings.'*
>
> *César Chávez, American labour leader*

Of course, I can't simply pluck an ethical relationship from thin air: this is how we ought to treat them – trust me! The legitimacy of the principles we follow in our dealings with familials depends on whether these principles can be derived from the basic moral case for animals, developed in the first chapter. There is, I shall try to show, a central ethical principle – the golden rule, if you like – governing human–familial relationships, and it can be derived from the basic moral case for animals. Let us remind ourselves of this case:

1 Animals count, morally speaking.

2 If something counts, morally speaking, then its most vital interests should not be sacrificed for the non-vital interests of others.

3 Therefore, we should not sacrifice the vital interests of animals for the non-vital interests of humans.

This argument has, in one way or another, underwritten most of the other arguments developed in this book, providing a framework within which we evaluate the practices of eating animals, experimenting on them, hunting them, and killing them for sport. How does it apply to the human–familial relationship?

▶ The Golden Rule

Suppose you have taken on the role of owner of, carer for, guardian of, or whatever (yes, I know, we need to come up with a decent name for one of those too) a familial animal. Then, incumbent in taking on this role is the following moral commitment:

The Golden Rule: *Do everything you can to promote the vital interests of your familial, as long as this does not involve sacrificing vital interests of your own.*

You are, of course, at liberty to promote your familial's non-vital interests, too: but that is something that is entirely up to you. (It is what moral philosophers call a *supererogatory action* – an action that goes above and beyond the call of duty.) The vital interests of both your familial and yourself come first. If the Golden Rule is correct, it is morally obligatory for you to promote your familial's vital interests in so far as you can, and in so far as this does not involve sacrificing similarly vital interests of your own. At the moment, however, this is just the skeleton of an idea. Let's put a little flesh on the bones.

Following the Golden Rule will, first, require that you know what vital interests your familial actually has. Doing so will involve both common sense and, where necessary, appropriate research. Which specific vital interests your familial has will, of course, depend on the type of animal it is. However, in general terms, your familial's vital interests will be broadly divisible into three sorts.

First, there are certain vital interests it will have purely by virtue of being a living creature. These will include access to (healthy, nutritious) food, water, shelter, security and suitable protection from either attack or misadventure, where these would result in bodily or emotional harm. These sorts of vital interests are species-neutral. They apply more or less equally to all

▲ Even the seemingly inoffensive practice of keeping family pets raises vexed ethical issues of animal rights.

species of animal. Some humans appear to think that these species-neutral vital interests are the only ones there are, or the only ones that count. A dog owner, for example, might ensure that their dog is properly fed, watered and protected. In doing this, they might feel that they are being a good owner. However, the dog spends its life languishing in the backyard: alone, bereft of company and meaningful stimulation. Its vital interests are not being taken care of because those interests are not restricted to the interests it has purely by virtue of being a living thing.

This brings us to the second type of vital interest: interests that a familial has in virtue of the type of familial it is – that is, in virtue of the species to which it belongs. These vital interests will vary from one species to another:

the vital interests of a dog will be very different from those of a goldfish. The species-specific vital interests of a dog derive from its intelligence and sociability. Prone to boredom, it needs exercise and stimulation, and an important facet of this stimulation will be the opportunity to interact with other creatures of its kind. In practical terms, promoting these vital interests will involve at least one long daily walk or run, preferably off its leash, in a place that affords social engagement.

Third, there are vital interests that attach to the individual animal itself, because of its history and character. Suppose, for example, that a dog is, for whatever reason, absolutely terrified of thunder, to the extent that it suffers significant emotional harm that is exacerbated when it is left on its own during a thunderstorm. Then, promoting the dog's vital interests requires taking steps to mitigate this. Perhaps some form of therapy will help the dog. If possible, arrangements might be made to ensure that the dog is not left on its own when a storm is likely. Other remedies might also be tried (for example, the provision of a dog crate where it might feel more comfortable). To leave it on its own without adequate provisions being made is a moral failure – a failure to respect a vital interest of the dog.

This, however, brings us to the second clause of the Golden Rule. This clause qualifies the extent to which one must promote the vital interests of one's familial. One is morally obligated to do so only if this does not involve sacrificing vital interests of one's own. The person who gives up their job, lives a meagre, spartan lifestyle, bereft of friends, for the sake of fully promoting their familial's vital interests is doing something that they are not morally required to do. Not all cases need be as extreme. It may be that your dog would benefit from a dog crate in order to alleviate its fear of thunder but it may also be that if you buy one you won't be able to eat for the next few days. You are not, of course, required to buy the crate.

However, in other cases, while promoting your familial's vital interests may be positively inconvenient or unpleasant, it may not involve sacrificing your vital interests. You may not feel like taking the dog for its daily walk. You've just got home from work, you're tired, it's cold and raining, and there's a show you want to see on TV. However, forcing yourself to go out for a walk, while a pain, is hardly sacrificing a vital interest – quite the contrary: it will do you good. Therefore, it seems, you are morally obliged to do it.

In some cases, it may be that your life makes sacrificing the vital interests of your familial inevitable. You work from early until late six days a week. Through no fault of your own, you really have no time to satisfy all of your familial's vital interests. You can try to change your life, but if that's not possible then the time may have come to question whether you really should have a familial in these circumstances. Of course, then you face the thorny problem of what to do. Most of the easy options (animal shelters) will make its life worse. So, morally speaking, the best option is to try to find it a home where its vital interests will be better met. If you sincerely try to do that, then, even if you fail, this is all that morality requires in this case.

In general, sharing one's life with a familial can be a delicate balancing act, one that involves trading off of vital and non-vital interest alike. To put it another way: sharing your life with a familial is an exacting moral discipline. It makes moral demands on you, and often these are difficult to meet. The most you can do is to try your best. But at the same time this is the least you can do.

▶ When good pets go bad

Animals, familial or otherwise, are not moral agents: they cannot be morally praised or blamed for what they do. Nevertheless, familials are implicated in a considerable amount of suffering. The number of birds killed by familial cats in the US has recently been estimated to be in the billions annually. Most familial animals eat other animals simply because their owners feed other animals to them, and in so doing add to the profits of the meat industry. A cat cannot subject its behaviour to critical moral scrutiny: 'I am inclined to hunt and kill this bird. Should I resist this inclination or should I embrace it?' This sort of reasoning process is, presumably, beyond the abilities of the average household cat. Nor can a dog agonize over whether the diet put in its bowl on a daily basis meets the most exacting moral requirements. But we – their owners, or whatever word we like to use to describe ourselves – can.

The standard by which what we do should be evaluated is a familiar one: Are the most vital interests of animals being sacrificed and, if so, are there any corresponding interests of animals being promoted? Your cat – Sylvester – likes his outdoor excursions. However, he does come back with a dead bird in his maw every now and then. The vital interests of the bird in question have clearly been sacrificed. Are there any similarly vital interests of the cat that are promoted? Arguably, there are. Perhaps a life stuck in a house or apartment is no life at all for a cat – notwithstanding the obvious dangers of the great outdoors. I don't know enough about cats to adjudicate. Nevertheless, even if you decide that spending time outdoors is a vital interest of Sylvester's, one possible solution is... bells. Making sure he has a bell on his collar drastically reduces his ability to kill birds (and mice and other animals). Compromise has been reached and for a minimal price – unless, of course, the bell makes the cat vulnerable to other animals that would do him harm, such as dogs.

The question of diet is also difficult. Some familials – notably cats – are widely thought of as *obligate* carnivores: animals that require meat in order to survive. However, this claim is controversial, and some companies – for example, Evolution Diet – make completely vegetarian food for cats (and dogs and ferrets). Without wishing to become embroiled in this dispute, we can say this: *If* it is true that cats need to eat meat to survive, then no moral argument can show that they should not eat meat. There may be a moral argument to the effect that one should not bring into existence creatures that eat meat. If valid, this argument would condemn cat keeping as morally wrong. But I am far from convinced this argument would be valid. At the root of this issue we find two different ways of thinking about morality. One view sees moral action as in the business of minimizing suffering (and perhaps maximizing happiness). From this perspective, the practice of cat keeping might be in trouble. But, on another way of thinking about morality, moral action is all about minimizing acts that are wrong (and maximizing acts that are right). If cats are, in fact, obligates carnivores, the cat must eat meat to survive. Therefore, no wrong is done when it eats meat. If so, then it can be argued (not necessarily successfully – but a case can be made) that the cat owner is doing nothing wrong in enabling his or her cat to eat meat. I'll talk more about this issue when I discuss predation (in Chapter 9). Whatever else is true, we need to remember that cats have a much stronger claim to eating meat than we do.

The case of dogs eating meat is more problematic because many dogs seem to be able to live happy, healthy lives on a vegetarian diet. Therefore, their eating meat seems to allow a non-vital interest of the dog to outweigh a vital interest of the cow, chicken, pig or (in all likelihood) horse they happen to eat. This is a tricky matter. Maintaining health on a vegetarian diet has been beyond more than a few humans I know. It takes a certain amount of care and planning. 'Egg and chips' vegetarians don't tend to thrive. But at least when you are on a vegetarian diet you have the kind of biological feedback from your own body that lets you know when you are not doing so well. The dog's biological feedback is not available to its owner. It is, perhaps, no easy thing to keep a dog healthy on a purely vegetarian diet. But this is not to say that it can't be done. And, if it can be done, it should be done. I think all responsible dog owners are under an obligation to try, but are under no obligation to persist if, despite their sincere and best efforts, it does not seem to be working.

9

Dog eat dog

'...we respect the vital interests of wild animals by treating them as citizens of sovereign territories.'

▶ The law of the jungle

There is a familiar objection to the idea of animal rights: Animals eat each other, so why shouldn't we eat them? There is an obvious response. Animals have no choice. If they didn't eat each other, they would die. We, on the other hand, do have a choice. We don't need to eat animals. For us, there is a range of alternative diets, and we can live happy, healthy lives on them. We can frame this idea in terms of the basic argument developed in Chapter 1. When one animal eats another, the vital interests of the eater are pitted against the similarly vital interests of the eaten. It is a vital interest of one animal to eat and a vital interest of the other not to be eaten. Both animals count, morally speaking. However, because of certain unfortunate facets of the way the world has been designed (specifically, the first and second laws of thermodynamics), satisfying the interests of one will necessitate violating the interests of the other. According to the basic argument, therefore, there is nothing morally wrong with one animal eating another.

This argument is, I think, faultless. Nevertheless, there are certain puzzles that it engenders, and these need to be addressed. First, suppose a lion is about to kill a gazelle. Swayed by the basic argument, we might reason as follows: there are the vital interests of the lion, and the vital interests of the gazelle, and, unfortunately, satisfying the former involves thwarting the latter. The basic argument says nothing about a situation like this. Therefore, there is no moral requirement that we intervene to save the gazelle. Therefore, there is no moral reason to save the gazelle. Very well: but suppose we now replace the gazelle with a child? We have the vital interests of the lion, and the similarly vital interests of the child. Do we really have no moral reason to save the child? This seems implausible. And, if we do have a reason to save the child, why do we not have a reason the save the gazelle? This is the first puzzle. I shall call it *the puzzle of the gazelle and the child.*

> *'Who trusted God was love indeed'*
> *And love Creation's final law*
> *Tho' Nature, red in tooth and claw*
> *With ravine, shriek'd against his creed*

Alfred Lord Tennyson, English poet

Second, predation is a rather ghastly affair, involving enormous, sometimes for us even unimaginable, suffering. For example, African wild dogs will sometimes kill wildebeest by biting their testicles and hanging on until the animal tires and eventually falls (my eyes are watering even as I type these words). Predation may be a fact of life, but it is a fact that is not immune to human intervention. We can't simply go around stymying the efforts of lions to catch gazelles, or wolves to catch caribou, of course. That would override the most vital interests of these animals. However, we might be able to intervene in other, subtler, ways. For example, predators could be painlessly eliminated by means of contraception, and the explosion of numbers in former prey animals could be controlled in the same way. To do this would be 'meddling with nature'. Nevertheless, it is a form of meddling that, if successful, would drastically reduce the amount of suffering in the world (just as, for example, did the 'meddling' that resulted in the elimination of the smallpox virus). So, if we could successfully meddle with the predator–prey relation, why shouldn't we do it? Let us call this *the puzzle of predation*.

Both these puzzles point in the direction of what I shall call *the sovereign territories model of predator–prey relations*. (I am indebted here to Donaldson & Kymlicka 2011.) This is not a rejection of the basic argument, but an acknowledgement that our moral relations to wild animals are not the same as those we bear to their domestic counterparts. The sovereign territories model, that is, provides an interpretation of how the basic argument should be applied in the case of wild animals.

▶ Sovereign territories

One way to respect the vital interests of a group of humans is to respect their right to self-determination. That is, we allow them to organize their societies on their own terms, and sort out the inevitable problems that arise in their own way. In exceptional circumstances, there may be a case for intervention. First, if the society is a clear and immediate threat to societies around it, there may be a case for intervention on general grounds of self-protection. Second, if there has been some sort of catastrophe so severe that it undermines the ability of the society to function or even continue in existence – drought, famine, disease and so on – then there might be a case for intervention on humanitarian grounds. In the absence of these factors, however, the case for intervention is at best uncertain. We may not like the way the society conducts itself and we may abhor its practices, but our attempts to change it will take the manifold forms of 'persuasion'.

Think of animal communities as forming sovereign territories in this sort of sense. Intervention in these societies would be justified if they posed a clear and immediate threat to humans. Most animal societies pose no such thing, of course. This condition would, however, justify our invention in the case of pathogens such as smallpox (even though bacteria and viruses are not animals – and it is not even clear that viruses are alive). Occasionally, there are catastrophes that jeopardize the existence or ability to function of the animal communities. In these circumstances, intervention might be justified – especially since these catastrophes are usually our work (oil spills, poaching that decimates populations, and so on). However, most of the time, intervention is not justified. Failure to intervene in these societies is not a failure to respect the vital interests of the members of these societies. It is an interpretation of what it means to respect their most vital interests.

With this sovereign territories model in mind, consider the puzzle of the gazelle and the child. We can justify intervention in this case on the grounds that the child is a member of our society – of our sovereign territory – who has inadvertently wandered into the sovereign territory of others. We want him back, in the same way that we might want back a hiker who had inadvertently wandered into the territory of a hostile nation. We might not be willing to start a war over it. But neither, in this case, are we proposing to wage a war on lions – always preventing them eating prey and things like that. If we can, stealthily, remove the boy from the lion's jaws, we are justified in doing so on the sovereign territories model. We would, for exactly the same reasons, be justified in saving the family dog if it should find itself in a similar situation.

Consider, now, the puzzle of predation. Predation is, as previously mentioned, a rather ghastly business and drastically increases the overall amount of suffering in the world. Suffering is a bad thing, and it seems to be the case that, as a general principle of morality, if we can eliminate bad things, then we probably should. In principle, we can at least reduce, maybe even eliminate, suffering caused by predation – and we can do it without causing further suffering. Suppose, for example, we could eliminate the predators by some sort of widespread contraception programme. How this could be done I have no idea. Perhaps we could crop-dust their territories with contraceptive powder, or we might do it one predator at a time, by tranquillizing them and compromising their reproductive systems. The point is that if we could – somehow – do this, thereby saving animals vast amounts of suffering, why shouldn't we do it? And if the numbers of the animals formerly known as prey explode, then we'll deal with them in the same way.

This, I assume, will strike many people as absurd. I am one of those people. But the absurdity is the point. If we think that animals count, morally speaking, aren't we ultimately committed to this absurd contraceptive-happy position? I suppose one could point out just how impractical this would be: how laborious and time-consuming, and just how many resources it would consume. If predators were painlessly eradicated, then the exploding numbers of prey would have to be controlled – in perpetuity. We would, in effect, be in the position of an occupying army whose occupation can never end. It is not a practical option, of course. But bemoaning its impracticality misses the point. It is a question of principle. The view that animals count, morally speaking, ultimately commits you to an absurd position – even if that position is only a matter of principle. And, therefore, the view that animals count morally is, itself, an absurd view. (The type of argument employed here is known as a *reductio ad absurdum*. Take a view, any view. Show that it entails an absurdity. This is enough to show that the view is, itself, absurd.)

The sovereign territories model allows us to resist this conclusion, thereby avoiding the charge of absurdity. The mooted grounds for this imagined intervention in nature would be the suffering of the animals preyed upon. The first point to note is that suffering does not, in general, provide a justification for intervention in a sovereign

▲ A lioness attacks a kudu – using the 'sovereign territories' model, human intervention to prevent the kudu's suffering is unjustified, even *un*ethical.

territory. It might form part of a justification but, typically, other justificatory factors need to be involved also.

▶ A justification for human intervention

Suppose we have two human societies: one of devout believers and the other of religious sceptics. Suppose, further, that numerous studies have confirmed that the believers are happier than the sceptics – much happier, in fact. When they reach a certain age, the sceptics realize that there is nothing in store for them after they die, and this realization is a source of great suffering for the majority of them. The believers feel sorry for them. If only, they say, we could convince them that death is not the end, they would be so much happier. Would the believers be justified in invading the society of sceptics, and forcibly changing their beliefs – maybe over the course of several generations so that the conversion can really take root? There is no plausible political theory that would claim that intervention is justified in this sort of case. Widespread suffering – even when this is severe and prolonged – does not, by itself, provide a case for intervention.

The further ingredients required to justify intervention can be of two sorts:

1 The suffering is produced by serious societal breakdown, perhaps the result of a catastrophic event from which the society is unable to recover on its own.

2 The suffering involves serious moral wrong: suffering is the result of a moral wrong being perpetrated by one group on another.

Neither of these conditions is satisfied in the case of animals. Predation is not the result of some catastrophe that undermines the ability to function of the sovereign animal territory. On the contrary, well-established predator–prey relations, in part, underwrite the proper functioning of that territory.

Neither is there any moral wrong being perpetrated by one group on another. When a lion eats a gazelle or a wolf eats a deer, the lion or wolf commits no moral wrong. This point is important. Morality is fundamentally about promoting what is right and preventing what is wrong. Suffering and/or happiness come into this only in so far as, in general, happiness is a good thing and suffering is a bad thing. It is clear that when a lion eats a gazelle it is doing nothing morally wrong. Even if we overlook the fact that the lion cannot morally evaluate what it is doing – 'I'm inclined to eat this gazelle. Is this an inclination I should endorse or resist?' is presumably not a thought that the lion is capable of thinking – there are vital interests of the lion at stake. If it doesn't eat meat, it will die. Therefore, no moral wrong is being committed by the lion on the gazelle when the former eats the latter. The suffering it causes in the process, while deeply unfortunate, is not a moral wrong that it inflicts on the gazelle. Morality is, fundamentally, a matter of promoting what is morally right and preventing what is morally wrong. Nothing morally wrong happens when one animal preys on another. Therefore, there is no moral case against predation.

In general, we respect the vital interests of wild animals by treating them as citizens of sovereign territories. Intervention in their affairs can be justified in more or less exceptional circumstances – the case of the lion and the child is one of those. But, in normal circumstances, intervention is not justified. We can, thankfully, keep our contraceptives to ourselves.

▶ Zoos

Zoos – zoological gardens – occupy a spectrum. At one extreme, if you see, for example, a wolf – a highly social mammal – living in isolation in a small concrete run, then you can be pretty sure that many of its most vital interests are being violated. At the other extreme are safari parks, where animals at least have room to roam and live in social groups. The general rule seems to be this: The more a zoo replicates natural conditions the less it violates the vital interests of the animals it contains. Correspondingly, of course, the less likely the animals in question will be readily visible to the paying customer – which is, of course, the primary purpose of zoos. So, the moral seems to be that the less a zoo violates the vital interests of animals, the more it undermines it own primary reason for existing, and vice versa. Perhaps there is some optimal trade-off – one that somehow preserves the vital interests of animals but also promotes the interests of the viewing customer. Even if there is – and it is far from clear where such a point would be – it is reasonably clear that most zoos do not achieve it. Safari parks certainly come closer to this optimal point than the average zoo. Whether they come close enough is open for debate.

Nor do there seem to be any vital human interests promoted by zoos. Education does not seem to require the presence of live animals, and on any trip around the local zoo it is often unclear what, if any, educational purpose is being achieved (or even attempted).

So zoos, in general, are probably not good things, morally speaking. A pity – my kids love the zoo.

The FAQs and only the FAQs

'The true moral test of humanity [...] lies in its relation to those who are at its mercy: the animals.'

Milan Kundera

Don't we have more important things to worry about than animals?

I assume the 'more important things to worry about' denotes humans, with their multifarious problems. Of course, worrying about humans and worrying about animals are hardly incompatible. The most important things we can do for animals are not so much things we do as things we don't do: not eating them, for example. If you want a longer list: not wearing fur or leather, not investing in companies that exploit animals, not buying cosmetics from companies that test on animals, and so on and so forth. These sorts of things are what philosophers call *negative obligations* as opposed to *positive obligations*. The latter actually take time and effort. Not so for the former: not doing something takes no time at all. If everyone exercised only his or her negative obligations with regard to animals, the world would be utterly transformed – for the better. Also, I refer you back to the discussion of the human costs of eating animals in Chapter 4. Not only does not eating animals take no time, it can also benefit humans immensely.

But aren't we natural meat eaters?

Sometimes, I hear it argued that we were 'destined to eat meat'. It is likely that the eating of meat once played an important role in human development, providing us with sufficient protein for our brains to undergo the sort of enormous growth – *encephalization* – that culminated in anatomically modern humans. However, just because something was once useful does not mean that it will always be so. There is, for example, one practice that seems to be common to the development of all civilizations and that thus arguably played a crucial role in the civilizing process: slavery. Even if this is true, however, it does not mean that slavery is now a good thing. Of course it is not. For much of the world, it is a practice that we have, thankfully, outgrown. To say that eating meat was once a good thing does not entail that it continues to be. Given the ready availability of high-quality vegetable proteins that can be produced at a fraction of the environmental cost, eating meat is now a very bad thing, both morally and prudentially.

What would happen to all the animals if we were to stop eating them?

One sometimes encounters a caricature of the idea that animals count morally: the gates of factory farms everywhere are flung open, and billions of homeless animals will be wandering the streets, starving and destitute. That is, of course, a caricature. A more sober proposal would be for the gradual phasing out of animal agriculture – over years or, more likely, decades. After this phasing out is complete there would, it goes without saying, be a lot fewer of these sorts of animals around. But that is OK. The welfare of an individual animal is not tied to the number of other animals there are of the same species. The land that is not taken up with pastoral farming could be returned to its wild state and so provide a home for various sorts of interesting creatures, including previously eradicated keystone predators. In my opinion, it would be nice to preserve the domestic pig, the dairy cow, the laying hen and other creatures that we used to exploit. If enough people feel like me, then it will be possible to set up sanctuaries where these

ALL THAT MATTERS: ANIMAL RIGHTS

animals can live happy, fulfilled and unabbreviated lives rather than the short, sharp nightmares they now have to endure.

What about the economic interests of those employed in the animal industry? Aren't they vital human interests?

Economic interests, in this sense, do not count as vital human interests. One can't justify slavery, for example, by appeal to the economic interests of the slave-owner. If a practice is morally wrong, one cannot appeal to economic considerations to justify it, and this is precisely because economic interests are not vital ones. There is a good reason for this. If you lose a job – as most people do at one time or another – then you can find another one. (In the meantime, having access to food and shelter is a vital interest of yours, and most systems of government in the developed world make allowance for this with some sort of welfare system.) Given that we are talking about a phasing out of animal agriculture over years or decades, those whose economic interests are bound up with it would have a luxury that few other workers enjoy: the luxury of having time to prepare for a new job or career.

What about *in vitro* meat? What do you think about that?

What do I think of meat grown in a laboratory? Short answer: yes, I'm all for it. Some animals will suffer, but a vanishingly small number compared to the current regime. The environmental impact is not absolutely certain, but it does look rather promising. So, I think this much is clear: a world where everyone ate *in vitro* meat would be a much, much, much better world than a world, like ours, where we eat – what shall we call it? – *in vivo* meat. It's a bit pricey at the moment, though – I think a burger will set you back about half a billion.

Speaking of pricey, isn't it more expensive to be a vegetarian?

No, it's cheaper.

But what about the essential amino acids? I need meat for those, don't I?

No, you just need to learn to combine your vegetables and legumes in the right way. There are numerous places on the Internet that will tell you how. This one is particularly good: http://www.nomeatathlete.com

OK, I've decided to try and stop eating meat. How do I go about it?

The instantly-becoming-vegan-at-the-stroke-of-midnight strategy works for some but others do better with baby steps. If you are one of those others, maybe you should try meatless Mondays. If everyone did that, consistently, then over time there would be a huge decrease in the overall amount of suffering in the world. Once you've got the hang of meatless Mondays, then try throwing in a meatless Friday, too. Every step you take increases, to use Marc Bekoff's useful expression, your 'compassion footprint'. The most important thing to realize is that you are on a journey, and some journeys take longer than others. Speaking of journeys...

It was going so well. But then I woke up one morning clinging determinedly to some ribs and covered in barbecue sauce. What should I do?

First, don't panic! You've had a relapse. Most of us have been there. Don't worry about it. Certainly, don't beat yourself up about it. Get up, dust yourself off, and get back upon the wagon. Acquiring a virtue is no easy business – and that is what you are doing: acquiring the virtue of *mercy*. In *The Unbearable Lightness of Being*, Milan Kundera writes:

> *True human goodness can manifest itself, in all its purity and liberty, only in regard to those who have no power. The true moral test of humanity (the most radical, situated on a level so profound it escapes our notice) lies in its relation to those who are at its mercy: the animals. And it is in that that exists the fundamental failing of man, so fundamental that all others follow from it.* (Kundera 1983; my translation)

Mercy, in this sense, is the virtue of taking the interests of all into account, even – indeed, especially – those who have no power. The virtue of mercy – and its corresponding vice, mercilessness – is peculiarly central among the virtues. Without mercy, it is not possible to have many of the other moral virtues. You are not an honest person if your honesty is directed only towards those who are as, or more, powerful than you. You are merely calculating. Neither are you kind, benevolent or loyal if your kindness, benevolence or loyalty extends only as far as those who are as, or more, powerful than you: you are merely self-serving. (I develop this virtue-ethical case further in Rowlands 2009: Chapter 5.)

Without the virtue of mercy, many – perhaps all – of the other moral virtues will escape us. Becoming ethical in our dealings with animals is, fundamentally, a matter of acquiring the virtue of mercy.

The acquisition of a virtue is no easy matter. I think Aristotle, writing in about 350 BCE, is right when he emphasizes the role of practice in its acquisition:

> *The virtues arise in us neither by nature not against nature. Rather, we are by nature able to acquire them, and we are completed through habit... Virtues we acquire just as we acquire crafts, by having first activated them. For we learn a craft by producing the same product that we must produce when we have learned it; we become builders, for example, by building, and we become harpists by playing the harp. Similarly, then, we become just by doing just actions, temperate by doing temperate actions, brave by doing brave actions.* (Aristotle 1999)

We become merciful by acting mercifully. Eventually, it will become second nature. But that is the culmination of a long and difficult process. If virtues were easy things to possess, everyone would have them. Be patient with yourself and be patient with other people, for in the end you have no choice. Have no truck with the 'if you're not a vegan you're a monster' attitude you find in some people. Everyone is flawed, everyone is fallible: even vegans. Doing the right thing is not easy, although some find it easier than others. Above all else, you are in the process of becoming better than you are. We must all become better than we are – me as much as anyone.

This **100 Ideas** section gives ways you can explore the subject in more depth. It's much more than just the usual reading list.

Ten famous dead vegetarians

1 **Siddhãrtha Gautama Buddha** The Enlightened one whose dictum was 'First do no harm'.

2 **(St) Francis of Assisi** Founder of the Franciscan order and patron saint of animals. He once blessed a wolf.

3 **Mahatma Gandhi** A vegetarian for most of his life, he wrote a book called *The Moral Basis of Vegetarianism*.

4 **Franz Kafka** Author of *The Trial* and *The Castle*. 'Now I can at least look at you in peace. I don't eat you anymore,' he once reportedly said to a fish.

5 **Pythagoras** One of the most prominent philosophers of the ancient world, he believed that abstaining from meat nurtured peace: '...for those who are accustomed to abominate the slaughter of other animals, as iniquitous and unnatural, will think it still more unjust and unlawful to kill a man or to engage in war'.

6 **George Bernard Shaw** Shaw became a vegetarian at 25 and remained so for his remaining 66 years.

7 **Percy Bysshe Shelley** 'If the use of animal food be, in consequence, subversive to the peace of human society, how unwarrantable is the injustice and the barbarity which is exercised toward these miserable victims. They are called into existence by human artifice that they may drag out a short and miserable existence of slavery and disease.'

8 **Albert Schweitzer** Nobel Prize-winning physician, theologian and vegetarian. 'The man who has become a thinking being feels a compulsion to give every will-to-live the same reverence for life that he gives to his own.'

9 **Leonardo da Vinci** Unequalled all-round genius, da Vinci was at least a vegetarian, possibly a vegan.

10 **Tolstoy, Leo** The author of *War and Peace* and *Anna Karenina* also wrote an essay defending vegetarianism entitled *The First Step*: 'This is dreadful... that people suppress in themselves, unnecessarily, the highest spiritual capacity – that of sympathy and pity towards living creatures like themselves – and by violating their own feelings, become cruel.'

Ten famous living vegetarians

11 **Casey Affleck** Actor and vegan. I thought he was very good in *Gone Baby Gone*.

12 **Pamela Anderson** There's more to this lady than meets the eye. She is a consistent and effective supporter of animal causes.

13 **Christian Bale** The Dark Knight was vegetarian from the age of seven, though he admits to falling off the wagon occasionally. Been there, bro'.

14 Bill Clinton Almost anyway – he does admit to 'a little fish once every now and then'. He was propelled into largely vegan ways by a quadruple bypass.

15 Billy Idol Nice day for a white wedding? Catering would have to be veggie.

16 Michael Imperioli Yes, Christopher Moltisanti of *The Sopranos* is vegan. You got a problem with that?

17 Sir Paul McCartney McCartney is a vocal supporter of animal causes. His late wife, Linda, through her well-known, 'accessible on every high street' vegetarian food range did as much as anyone to advance the cause of animals.

18 Ian McKellen Yay, Gandalf is a veggie, too!

19 Natalie Portman Superb at playing a Black Swan, but you won't find her eating one.

20 Alicia Silverstone Actress star of *Clueless* and bestselling author of *The Kind Diet*.

Ten vegetarian athletes

21 Mac Danzig Mixed martial artist and winner of Ultimate Fighter and former King of the Cage lightweight world champion. A vegan since 2004.

22 Scott Jurek Arguably the greatest ultrarunner ever, Jurek won the Hardrock once, the Badwater twice, the Spartathlon three times, and the Western States 100 seven times. He's a vegan.

23 Carl Lewis The nine-time Olympic Gold medallist was a vegan at the time of his 1991 World Championships triumph – which he rates as the best competition of his career.

24 Edwin Moses The two-time Olympic 400-metres hurdles champion and world-record holder is a vegetarian.

25 Joe Namath One of the greatest quarterbacks ever. His most famous quote is, perhaps, 'We're going to win, I guarantee it', said before the 1969 Super Bowl. Here is a lesser-known one: 'I have been a vegetarian for a few years. Fred Dryer of the Rams has been one for ten years. It shows you don't need meat to play football.'

26 Martina Navratilova Vocal supporter of PETA (People for the Ethical Treatment of Animals) and possibly the greatest female tennis player ever (along with Billie Jean King, also a vegetarian).

27 Paavo Nurmi The 'Flying Finn' set 20 world records in distance running and won nine Olympic medals. Vegetarian.

28 Dave Scott The first six-time triathlon world champion – known as 'The Man' – was vegan at the time of his competitive peak.

29 Mike Tyson Formerly the 'baddest man on the planet' and now a pigeon-fancying vegan. Quite a spiritual journey this man has been on. But I bet Evander Holyfield wished Mike had become a vegan a little earlier.

30 Freddie Welsh Lightweight boxing champion of the world at a time where the expression 'world champion' means more than it does today. Vegetarian.

Five famous fictional vegetarians

31 Frankenstein's Monster Yes he was. Read the book.

32 Mr Spock The Vulcan First Officer of the *Enterprise* – not the child psychologist, *Dr* Spock (although he was a vegetarian, too).

33 Lisa Simpson Homer's idealistic daughter is one of two vegetarian characters in *The Simpsons*, the other being Dr Apu Nahasapeemapetilon.

34 Superman As revealed in *Superman: Birthright* in 2003. When not occupied fighting the mighty Zod, he has been known to advertise peanut butter.

35 Elle Woods Sorority girl turned legal hotshot in *Legally Blonde*. Her dog was also vegetarian, though perhaps not through choice.

Five great books on animal rights

36 Marc Bekoff, *The Animals Manifesto: Six Reasons for Expanding our Compassion Footprint* (Novato, CA: New World Library, 2010)

37 Andrew Linzey, *Animal Theology* (Chicago: University of Illinois Press, 1994)

38 Tom Regan, *The Case for Animal Rights* (Berkeley, CA: University of California Press, 1983)

39 Jonathan Safran Foer, *Eating Animals* (New York: Little Brown, 2009)

40 Peter Singer, *Animal Liberation* (New York: HarperCollins, 1975)

Five great vegetarian/vegan cookbooks

41 Natasha Corrett and Vicki Edgson, *Honestly Healthy: Eat with Your Body in Mind, the Alkaline Way* (London: Jacqui Small, 2012)

42 Dennis Cotter, *The Café Paradiso Cookbook* (Cork: Atrium, 1999)

43 Ross Dobson, *Market Vegetarian* (New York: Ryland Peters and Small, 2008)

44 Mark Reinfeld and Jennifer Murray, *The Thirty Minute Vegan* (Cambridge, MA: Da Capo Press, 2009)

45 Alicia Silverstone, *The Kind Diet: A Simple Guide to Feeling Great, Losing Weight, and Saving the Planet* (New York: Rodale, 2009)

Ten influential animal organizations

46 **PETA** (People for the Ethical Treatment of Animals)

www.peta.org

47 **Defenders of Wildlife**

www.defenders.org

48 **WSPA** (World Society for the Protection of Animals)

http://www.wspa-international.org/

49 **BUAV** (British Union for the Abolition of Vivisection)

www.buav.org

50 **CIWF** (Compassion in World Farming)

www.ciwf.org.uk

51 **World Wildlife Federation**

http://worldwildlife.org/

52 **RSPCA** (Royal Society for the Prevention of Cruelty to Animals)

http://www.rspca.org.uk/home

100 Ideas

53 ASPCA (American Society for the Prevention of Cruelty to Animals)

http://www.aspca.org/

54 HSUS (Humane Society of the United States)

http://www.humanesociety.org/

55 IFAW (International Fund for Animal Welfare)

http://www.ifaw.org/united-states

Ten useful websites

56 No Meat Athlete

www.nomeatathlete.com

57 The Animal Rights FAQ

www.animal-rights.com

58 Animal Rights – Wikipedia article

http://en.wikipedia.org/wiki/Animal_rights

59 Animal Rights – About.com article

http://animalrights.about.com/

60 Marc Bekoff's blog at *Psychology Today*

http://www.psychologytoday.com/blog/animal-emotions

61 Oxford Centre for Animal Ethics

http://www.oxfordanimalethics.com/

62 Animal Rights: The Abolitionist Approach

http://www.abolitionistapproach.com/

63 Vegan Cooking

http://www.vegancooking.com/

64 Vegan Society

http://www.vegansociety.com/

65 The Vegetarian Society

https://www.vegsoc.org/

Ten species near extinction (range / numbers remaining in the wild / cause)

66 Javan rhinoceros (Indonesia and Vietnam / 60 / poaching and habitat loss)

67 Golden-headed langur (Vietnam / 70/ habitat loss)

68 Vaquita (Gulf of California /2–300 / overfishing)

69 Cross River gorilla (Nigeria, Cameroon / fewer than 300 / hunting and deforestation)

70 Sumatran tiger (Sumatra / fewer than 600 / hunting and habitat loss)

71 Mekong giant catfish (South-East Asia / fewer than 1,000 / overfishing)

72 Black-footed ferret (North American Plains / fewer than 1,000 / habitat loss)

73 Borneo pygmy elephant (Northern Borneo / fewer than 1,500 / habitat loss)

74 Giant panda (China, Burma, Vietnam / fewer than 2,000 / habitat loss)

75 Polar bear (circumpolar Arctic / fewer than 25,000 / habitat loss)

Fifteen animals hunted to extinction (date of extinction)

76 Dodo (1680s)

77 Stellar's sea cow (1760s)

78 Great auk (1844)

79 Sea mink (1860s)

80 Atlas bear (1870s)

81 Falkland Island wolf (1876)

82 Quagga (1883)

83 Passenger pigeon (1896)

84 Bubal hartebeest (1923)

85 Tasmanian tiger (1930s)

86 Carolina parakeet (1939)

87 Toolache wallaby (1939)

88 Caspian tiger (1950s)

89 Zanzibar leopard (1990s)

90 Caribbean monk seal (2008)

Ten things you can do to make a difference

91 Become a vegetarian (or, better, vegan).

92 Refuse to buy products tested on animals.

93 Refuse to buy leather and fur.

94 Avoid investing in companies that exploit animals.

95 Educate yourself about animal issues.

96 Tell your family and friends (or anyone who will listen) about your beliefs – but do try not to be a bore.

97 Put your name to email campaigns against animal abuse. (And at the bit where they invite you to provide comments, always be polite – or you might find yourself on a no-fly list).

98 Write books and articles.

99 Give talks at schools, public meetings, etc.

100 Demonstrate, picket and protest (peacefully and legally) at appropriate sites.

Acknowledgements

The author and publisher would like to thank the following for permission to reproduce the following photographs: **Chapter 1** Milking parlour © Visuals Unlimited, Inc/Nigel Cattlin/Getty Images **Chapter 2** Badger © Thinkstock/Getty Images **Chapter 3** Bentham © Popperfoto/Getty Images **Chapter 4** Pig farm © Thinkstock/Getty Images **Chapter 5** Animal testing © Thinkstock/Getty Images **Chapter 6** Wolves © Ocean/Corbis Images **Chapter 7** Bullfight © Daniel Perez Garcia-Santos/Getty Images **Chapter 8** Dog walk © Thinkstock/Getty Images **Chapter 9** Lioness and kudu © Gallo Images

References

American Dietetic Association, 2009. 'Vegetarian diets', *American Dietetic Association* 109/7 (July 2009), pp. 1266–82.

APHIS 2005. http://www.aphis.usda.gov/animal_welfare/downloads/awreports/awreport2005.pdf

Aristotle 1999. Aristotle, *Nicomachean Ethics*, trans. T. Irwin (Indianapolis: Hackett, 1999), 1103a19–b2.

ASPCA 2013. American Society for Prevention of Cruelty to Animals, http://www.aspca.org/about-us/faq/pet-statistics.aspx

Bailey et al. 2005. J. Bailey et al., 'The future of teratology research is *in vitro*', *Biogenic Amines* 19/2 (2005), pp. 97–145.

Bekoff 2012. Marc Bekoff, 'Animals are conscious and should be treated as such', *New Scientist*, 26 Sept. 2012.

CDC 2007. The Centre for Disease Control, http://www.cdc.gov/healthypets/health_benefits.htm

Daily Mail 2012. 'Dogs destined for the table: Horrific images show animals being killed, cooked and served up as a meal in Chinese tradition', *Daily Mail*, 25 June 2012.

Donaldson & Kymlicka 2011. Sue Donaldson and Will Kymlicka, *Zoopolis: A Political Theory of Animal Rights* (Oxford University Press, 2011).

EFPIA 2011. European Federation of Pharmaceutical Industries and Associations, http://animalresearchforlife.eu/index.php/en/figures

Eisnitz 2006. Gail Eisnitz, *Slaughterhouse: The Shocking Story of Greed, Neglect, and Inhumane Treatment inside the U.S. Meat Industry* (New York: Prometheus Books, 2006).

Enterline 1988. P. Enterline, 'Asbestos and cancer', in L. Gordis (ed.), *Epidemiology and Health Risk Assessment* (New York: Oxford University Press, 1988).

Eshel & Martin 2006. Gideon Eshel and Pamela Martin, 'Diet, energy and global warming', *Earth Interactions* 10 (2006), Paper 1. Available at http://earthinteractions. org/; find the article via the site search button.

FAO 2006a. Food and Agriculture Organization of the United Nations, Livestock, Environment, and Development Initiative, 'Livestock's long shadow: environmental issues and options', http://www.fao.org (ftp://ftp.fao.org/docrep/fao/010/a0701e/a0701e00.pdf)

FAO 2006b. Food and Agriculture Organization of the United Nations, 'Livestock a major threat to environment', http://www.fao.org/newsroom/en/news/2006/1000448/index.html

FDA 2004. U.S. Food and Drug Administration, *Critical Pathway Report: Challenges and Opportunities*, March 2004. Available at http://www.fda.gov/ScienceResearch/SpecialTopics/CriticalPathInitiative/CriticalPathOpportunitiesReports/ucm077262.htm

Feinberg 1970. Joel Feinberg, 'The nature and value of rights', *Journal of Value Inquiry* 4 (1970), pp. 243–60.

Fiske-Harrison 2011. Alexander Fiske-Harrison, *Into the Arena* (Profile Books, 2011).

Francione 2007. Gary Francione, 'Animal rights and domesticated nonhumans' (blog), http://www.abolitionistapproach.com/animal-rights-and-domesticated-nonhumans/

Garrett 2012. J. Garrett (ed.), *The Ethics of Animal Experimentation* (Cambridge, MA: MIT Press, 2012).

Grady 2001. Denise Grady, 'Scientists see higher use of antibiotics on farms', *New York Times*, 8 Jan. 2001. Available at http://www/nytimes.com/2001/01/08/us/scientists-see-higher-use-of-antibiotics-on-farms.html

Hau, Svendson and Schapiro 1994. Jann Hau, Per Svendson and Steven Schapiro (eds), *Handbook of Laboratory Animal Science, Volume II, Animal Model* (CRC Press, 1994).

HSUS 2007. Humane Society of the United States, 'An HSUS report: human health implications of non-therapeutic antibiotic use in animal agriculture'. www.hsus.org; find the report via the site search button.

Hume 1975. David Hume, *A Treatise of Human Nature* [1739–40], ed. L. Selby-Bigge (Oxford University Press, 1975).

Klausner 1998. R. Klausner, *The Press*, 8 May 1998, p. 5.

Kundera 1983. Milan Kundera, *L'Insoutenable Legèreté de l'être* [The Unbearable Lightness of Being] (Paris: Gallimard, 1983).

Lab Animal 2001. *Lab Animal* 30/6 (June 2001), p. 13.

Lave 1988. Lester B. Lave et al., 'Information value of the rodent bioassay', *Nature* 336 (15 Dec. 1988), pp. 631–3.

Leaf 2004. C. Leaf, 'Why we are losing the war on cancer – and how to win it', *Fortune Magazine*, 22 Mar. 2004.

Lim et al. 2006. U. Lim et al, 'Prospective study of aspartame-containing beverages and risk of hematopoietic and brain cancers', 97th meeting of the American Association for Cancer Research, abstract 4010, 4 Apr. 2006.

MRMC 2006. Medical Research Modernization Committee, 'A critical look at animal experimentation', http://www.mrmcmed.org/Critcv.html, p. 4.

NCB 2005. Nuffield Council on Bioethics, 'The ethics of research involving animals', http://www.nuffieldbioethics.org/animal-research

Northrup 1957. E. Northrup, *Science Looks at Smoking* (New York: Coward-McCann, 1957).

O'Neill 2000. S. O'Neill et al., 'Progressive infection in a subset of HIV-1 positive chimpanzees', *Journal of Infectious Diseases* 182/4 (2000), pp. 1051–62.

PFMA 2012. Pet Food Manufacturers Association, http://www.pfma.org.uk/pet-population/

Pories et al. 1993. S. Pories et al., 'Animal models for colon carcinogenesis', *Archives of Surgery* 128 (1993), pp. 647–53.

PPA 2012. Pet Products Association, http://www.americanpetproducts.org/press_industrytrends.asp

Racaniello 2009. Vincent Racaniello, 'Ebola in pigs – Nipah redix, http://www.virology.ws/2009/01/26/ebola-in-pigs-nipah-redux/

Rowlands 2002. Mark Rowlands, *Animals Like Us* (London: Verso, 2002).

Rowlands 2009. Mark Rowlands, *Animal Rights: Moral Theory and Practice, 2nd edn* (Basingstoke: Macmillan, 2009).

Safran Foer 2009. Jonathan Safran Foer, *Eating Animals* (New York: Penguin, 2009).

Scruton 1996. Roger Scruton, *Animal Rights and Wrongs* (London: Demos, 1996).

Tauberberger et al. J. K. Tauberberger, Ann H. Reid, Raina M. Lourens, Ruixue Wang, Guozhong Jin and Thomas G. Fanning, 'Characterization of the 1918 influenza virus polymerase genes', *Nature* 437 (6 Oct. 2005), pp. 889–93.

UK Census 2011. Office of National Statistics, Statistical Bulletin: '2011 Census: Population Estimates for the United Kingdom, 27 March 2007', http://www.ons.gov.uk/ons/dcp171778_292378.pdf

UCS 2001. Union of Concerned Scientists, 'Hogging it! Estimates of antimicrobial abuse in livestock', 7 Apr. 2004. Report available at http://www.ucsusa.org; find the report via the site search button.

US Census Bureau 2012. US Census Bureau, US and World Population Clocks, http://www.census.gov/main/www/popclock.html (accessed 21 Dec. 2012)

WHO 2005. World Health Organization, 'Ten things you need to know about pandemic influenza', 2005, http://www.who.int/wer/2005/wer8049/en/

Zamir 2007. Tzachi Zamir, *Ethics and the Beast: A Speciesist Argument for Animal Liberation* (Princeton, NJ: Princeton University Press, 2007).

Index

ALL THAT MATTERS: ANIMAL RIGHTS

About the author

Mark Rowlands is Professor of Philosophy at the University of Miami. He took his doctorate from Oxford University and has held academic positions in Britain, France, Ireland and the US. Today he is one of the world's leading philosophers of animal rights.

Mark's best-known book is *The Philosopher and the Wolf* (2008), charting a decade of Mark's life that he spent living with a wolf. Dan Schneider described it as 'one of the great texts in modern English', the *Daily Mail* called it 'An extraordinary memoir', and the *Financial Times* said it was 'this year's most original and instructive work of popular philosophy'.

Also published in the ALL THAT MATTERS series:

PHILOSOPHY
by Julian Baggini

MUHAMMAD
by Ziauddin Sardar

BIOETHICS
by Donna Dickenson

GOD
by Mark Vernon

JUDAISM
by Keith Kahn-Harris

SUSTAINABILITY
by Chris Goodall

BUDDHISM
by Pascale Engelmajer

WATER
by Paul L. Younger

LOVE
by Mark Vernon

EUTHANASIA
By Richard Huxtable

HUMAN RIGHTS
by Ivan Fiser

POLITICAL PHILOSOPHY
by Johanna Oksala

CLASSICAL WORLD
by Alastair J.L. Blanshard

DEMOCRACY
by Steven Beller

FEMINISM
by Samantha Lyle

HISTORY OF MEDICINE
by Tim Hall

CYBER CRIME & WARFARE
by Peter Warren & Michael
Streeter

SPACE EXPLORATION
by David Ashford

FUTURE
by Ziauddin Sardar

THE ROMANS
by John Manley

MODERN CHINA
by Jonathan Clements

SHAKESPEARE'S TRAGEDIES
by Mike Scott

SHAKESPEARE'S COMEDIES
by Mike Scott

PLATO
by Ieuan Williamns

THE AUTISTIC SPECTRUM
by Lorna Selfe

INTERNATIONAL RELATIONS
by Ken Booth

THE RENAISSANCE
by Michael Halvorson

ANCIENT EGYPT
by Barry Kemp